JOSEPH SMITH

AND

OUR DESTINY

A Brief Vital Story of
God's Covenant Race from Patriarchal
Times to the Present

PUBLISHED BY EARL W. HARMER
1177 Yale Avenue — Salt Lake City 5, Utah
1965

LITHOGRAPHED IN U.S.A.
BY

PUBLISHERS PRESS

SALT LAKE CITY, UTAH

PREFACE TO PREVIOUS EDITIONS

In an article dated Sept. 3rd, 1940, millions of copies of which were distributed, Walter Lippmann blames our national education for the "Moral Unpreparedness" of the U. S. A., and goes on to say: "The teaching of politics and history in American colleges has, for the most part, been emptied of all the elements of greatness—that is to say of the conviction that history is not the meaningless tale of a race of mercenary idiots but the record of great men and great peoples, struggling indomitably to rise out of sloth and squalor.

"So the young men of our generation have been deprived of their birthright, which is to be conscious that they are the children of a high destiny, in the line of great men who performed great deeds, members of the noble company throughout the centuries who had faith when men were hopeless, who fortified reason against unreason, vindicated justice against violence, and in the jungle of animal passion cleared the spaces where the air is free and clear and tranquil. No people can be equal to its fate unless it has the consciousness of greatness. The consciousness of greatness can be preserved only by the memory of greatness; his sense of history is the secret magic by which Churchill is leading his people in this noblest and most glorious moment in the life of Great Britain. Our own historians, who think they have explained the greatness of the American past when they have explained it away, have emptied American history of all significant meaning, of its value as a source of wisdom, of its power to teach by example.

"The fact is that no nation can live and remain a nation if the people in it cease to remember and no longer respect their own history. For the American nation in particular—because it is still a new nation in the process of being formed out of many older nations—the common consciousness of a great past is indispensable. Without it, with no sense that there is an historic destiny in which Americans participate, with only the feeling that nothing great was ever done here and that American history is no more than the story of men on the make, this nation will never cohere. It will crumble into factions of self-seeking individuals. It will take refuge in cynicism and it will escape into sentimentality. It will go to sleep and then wake up in a panic; it will be complacent and frightened. It will never find, without the deep conviction that it is continuing a great history, either the unity which will make it secure or the hard, unconquerable spirit which, if it is tested, will make it victorious."

It is true "that no nation can live and remain a nation if the people in it lose the common consciousness of a great past", it is equally true that a church such as ours must be vitalized and sustained by the same sure foundation. God knew the profound import of both these facts when He instructed Lehi and his Book of Mormon colony to secure their historical and genealogical record on the brass plates as a basis for their future national and religious life. The later colony of Mulekites suffered a fatal national and religious decline for want of this very thing. The recorded history of these two Book of Mormon nations is both the positive and negative proof of the truth of Mr. Lippmann's statement.

The Church of Jesus Christ of Latter-day Saints has been very careful to preserve and teach its history from the days of Joseph Smith until now. Many of the younger members of the Church, however, have not come to understand the profound relationship between our Latter

Day history and the great drama of God's dealings with our fathers before the Restoration of the Gospel.

It is the sincere hope of the compiler of this book that its contents may assist the youth of our Church to better realize this, their ancient glorious past, with its great heritage and destiny. If our youth can see this actual, racial and historical relationship between Bible times and themselves it will measurably increase their faith in every phase of the restored gospel. With the exception of our Lord Jesus Christ no man ever laid claim to a greater manifestation of the divine power than did Joseph Smith. If his claims are correct it is only logical to expect that a century after his time the expanding volume of true history would begin to sustain and vindicate his work. That is exactly what is happening, and a growing vital faith in our claims to priesthood leadership, temple work, etc., can be obtained by a careful study of our marvelous racial and historical background.

The first section of this vital story covers the times from our fathers Abraham, Isaac and Jacob to the birth of the U.S.A. They were written by the well-known W. J. Cameron for the magazine "Destiny." Coming from such an outstanding non-L.D.S. source they may and should have added weight with those inclined to be skeptical of all Latter-day Saint effort to vindicate the teachings of the Church of Jesus Christ of Latter-day Saints.

The second section and pedigree chart are selections from "God's Covenant Race" by James H. Anderson, suggesting some of the profound relationships of Joseph Smith and the Latter-day Saints to our great racial past and our glorious destiny.

PREFACE — 1962-1965 EDITIONS

World history has moved switfly in the directions indicated in the first editions of this book. After reading them, many people have been able to view the coming storm calmly in the light of God's wisdom. These people have continually asked me for additional copies that might be used as gifts to friends or family. Upon their recommendation many other requests have also been made for this treasured presentation of the truth. These are some of the gratifying reasons for this third edition.

The occasion, also, has made it possible to enlarge the work through the addition of selected passages from Edward W. Tullidge's "Life of Joseph the Prophet," published in 1878. In his preface Tullidge says, "In its compilation I have been placed under obligation to the Hon. Joseph F. Smith and Eliza R. Snow (Smith) who kindly read and revised the manuscript."

"The late President (Brigham) Young requested me to write this book, and the late Apostle George A. Smith, on his death bed charged me solemnly concerning it. Its production therefore has been both a work of duty and affection."

He further adds, "Whenever I have had occasion to incorporate any portion of his (Joseph Smith's) many and voluminous revelations the endeavor has been to set them in their proper historical connections and surroundings, as only in such a presentation are some of them clear to the reader."

With this thinking I heartily agree. It is only when Joseph Smith is viewed in the historical perspective of many centuries that he becomes the right man, in the right place, at the right time and with the right message for the world in these latter days.

God is at work in the world today as in Bible times. In fact, these are Bible times in the sense that we as Israel, are fulfilling ancient God-given prophecies.

This new section written at the request of, and approved by, President Brigham Young, Apostle George Q. Cannon, Eliza R. Snow (Smith), wife of the Prophet Joseph and The Honorable Joseph F. Smith; added to the writings of James H. Anderson (Section 2) First Secretary of the Utah Genealogical Society; and W. J. Cameron (Section 1) nationally known non-LDS student of the House of Israel; reveals the golden thread that ties the present generations of Israel and their great Israel Prophet, Joseph Smith, to the past and the gloriously future ages.

As many a reader has said, "This book has given me a reason for the hope that is within me."

It can do the same for you. I hope it will.

Earl W. Harmer, Publisher

SECTION 1

Mr. W. J. Cameron was a well known automotive business man, radio speaker and president of the American Federation.

The Present Crisis

Once to every man and nation
   Comes the moment to decide,
In the strife of truth with falsehood,
   For the good or evil side;
Some great cause, God's new Messiah
   Offering each the bloom or blight,
And the choice goes by forever
   'Twixt that darkness and that light.

New occasions teach new duties;
   Time makes ancient good uncouth;
They must upward still, and onward,
   Who would keep abreast of truth;
Lo, before us gleam her camp-fires!
   We ourselves must pilgrims be,
Launch our Mayflower, and steer boldly
   Through the desperate winter sea,
Nor attempt the future's portal
   With the past's blood-rusted key.

           —James Russell Lowell.

IS THERE A CHOSEN PEOPLE?

By W. J. Cameron, Detroit, Michigan—1933 A. D.

I am to speak to you today on The Chosen People and their significance in the world. The text-book of this study is our oldest racial document, a library of 66 thin pamphlets to which is given the name of Bible. The thread which binds these five and a half dozen works in one, is the story of a race and its special place and work in the world. In presenting this Bible, I do not require that you approach it with any theory in its character as an inspired book. Inspiration is not an idea we **bring to** the Bible to give it an impressive supernatural standing; inspiration is an idea we fetch away from the Bible after we have somewhat sensed its unique inspiring character. No one can know that anything is inspired until it inspires him. Thus the Bible must remain an uninspired book to multitudes, regardless of their theory and creed, no matter how much they may profess to believe in its inspiration, because they have not experienced its inspiration. And by the same token the Bible is always being rediscovered as an inspired book because its penetrating, communicable livingness is continually being experienced afresh by old and new readers and by new generations.

The Bible labors under the disadvantage of being regarded as primarily a religious book. Yet you go a long way in the Bible before coming upon anything that savors of religion. It begins with geology and astronomy, meterology and biology, anthropology and psychology—all the materials of the physical and mental sciences, the concepts of time and space and motion, of creative method and purpose and progress. It has far less theology than most people imagine. Of course, God is central, but God is not a religious character. Certainly God is not an ecclesiastical character. The creating and sustaining God of the Bible and history appears as the sole competent Personality, the one completely Normal Being, of eternal wisdom, power and purpose, Who upholds all things by His spirit. It is a thousand pities that the inclusive thought of God should have suffered in men's minds by being mixed with an exclusive thought of religion. Religion appears in the Bible only after man's unnatural, sinful departure from God's naturalness; that is, religion, appears as an emergency element, a rescue force brought in because of abnormal human breakdown. And when it fulfills its part in the work of restoration, it will disappear. The last New Testament seer foresaw the distant future under the figure of heaven, and he wrote, "I saw no temple therein." Religion, as we know it, had fulfilled its purpose. The original plan of God had been restored. There was only God and the people.

Americans Are a Very Old Race

Now, in the matter of race there is much careless talk. We speak of "superior race" in a boastful tone. The Gentile boasts his superiority over the Jew, the Jew over the Gentile. The Prussian in Germany over the Saxon. The Dane over the Swede. The Parsee, descendant of royal Persians, over the various peoples of India. The Japanese (who have no idea of their own origin) over the Chinese. And so on. We Americans are accustomed to say that we are "a **new** race." Englishmen insist that we **are** "a new race," as if the branch that grows over the wall is not as old as the branch that hangs over the garden. Both branches are as old as the tree that bears them. Their roots are the same. We Americans are as old as our roots. We are indeed a very old race, much older than our American nation, older than the settlement in England, older than our first appearance in Europe. And never a barbarous or an enslaved race! The true effect of race knowledge is not to feed our vanity, or rouse our boastfulness; rather, it should arouse a profound sense of responsibility. Race has a great significance for the moral sanity and purpose of the individual.

We should not speak carelessly of race. It means

too much. For example: Moses, as you will remember. started out to be a reformer, and failed because he used force as his method, and he fled out of Egypt into the land of Midian. And there one day at a well he courteously helped some shepherdesses to water their flocks. The task took them so much less than the usual amount of time that when they returned home their father asked them, "How is it ye are come so soon today?" And they said. "An Egyptian drew water for us and watered the flock." Had these young women been correct in their racial deductions, it would have altered everything. **Moses was not an Egyptian.** Else he had never become the great Law-giver and the leader of Israel, and we should never have heard of him or of those girls at the watering well. **Moses was of Israel,** and that racial fact made all the difference.

Today especially we feel a revulsion against speaking of race at all. We dislike drawing invidious distinctions between people, as some feel they must do if they open the subject of race. Many do not know how to discuss this fact except upon a formula of marking other races down. And we see in other countries to what hideous conditions such a course can lead. But all of this simply indicates some basic lack of knowledge in ourselves. I lay it down as a rule that whenever the thought of race leads us to boastfulness or contempt, there is something false in it.

Nevertheless, race is a great fact and cannot be evad-ed. It is here. Men belong to various races, as trees be-long to different varieties. The races are different and they do fulfill different destinies. I am not speaking of na-tionalities. National divisions are largely artificial, they are constantly changing and with the increase of civiliza-tion will tend more and more to disappear. But race is not artificial; it is a basic natural fact. Take the Anglo-Saxon, for example, a distinct and easily distinguishable race. You will find Saxons who call themselves Germans or Bohemians; and in France, Frenchmen; and in Holland, Dutchmen; and in northern Europe, Scandinavians; and in England, Britons. All belong to one race stream, but divided by national names and language. Yet touch them on the intrinsic racial nerve, and their response to Liberty, Reverence, Orderly Social Life and Progress, are everywhere the same. The same ancestral voices speak in them. Take the United States and Canada—two nations of one blood, who before the Revolution were one nation. Do their national divisions really divide them in the things that matter? Not in the least.

The Pilgrim's March of the Ages

Now, whatever appears in life appears also in this Bible. Race is one of the most indelible natural facts, and, race is one of the most insistent Biblical facts. The Bible is not a history of the human race at large, but of one distinct people amongst the family of races, and all the other races are considered with reference to it. This painfully irks critics like Mr. H. G. Wells who thinks the Bible should be rewritten to include all the races of antiquity with their religions. If this Book were the history of the human race at large, of course that is the way it should be written. But the Bible is not ancient history; it is contemporary chronicle. It has nothing to do with dead races and dead religions, but with the race and religion that were to flow and widen and deepen to the end of the stream-bed of time. The Bible is not a treatise, but a panorama which moves to the mighty music of the Pilgrims' March of the ages. You will find no disquisitions upon history in all its pages, no metaphysical speculations upon the nature of the soul and the Beyond of Death; you will find a contemporary panorama of life and the soul; it spreads out the things itself before our eyes. This Book deals with one race which flows like a Gulf Stream through the ocean of humanity, and as that Gulf Stream touches two continents and blesses the nations, so this race in its origin, history and destiny was selected and equipped for the service of the nations. If any book can be called a racial book, it is the Bible. And the racial question will never be properly stated and its meaning will never be found, except on Biblical principles.

"But why should race appear in the Bible at all?" some may ask; "Is not God equally the God of all men?" Race is not in the Bible in the sense that the Bible can or does decree anything concerning it. Race is in life. This Book explains what has been done and why, shows us the thing in process. God writes no books. God writes in life. When He would show us oakness, He does not write a botanical or chemical formula—He makes an oak tree. God's choicest writing tablets are Peoples and Races. His original manuscript for us is our race, and the Bible gives us the highest reading of that manuscript that has been made. Our Lord Jesus Christ followed the same method. He wrote nothing. He left no book or creed or written rules behind Him. Twelve living men were his manuscripts. Upon them the Holy Spirit wrote His message, graved it on the tablets of the soul, planted it in the racial blood-stream—more imperishable than inscribed parchment or sculptured granite. In doing this, Our Lord followed the divine method, such a method as only a Divine Author can use.

A Fact That Cannot be Ignored

The race to whose story our Bible is largely devoted is called "The Chosen People." On this very point more people part company with the Bible than on any other point, except it be the moral law. It is a rather difficult situation, for people do not deny that a Chosen People is written there, in the plainest words, over and over again, from Genesis to Revelation—they do not deny it, they coolly ignore it as a point of no importance. And yet, if it be true not only in the Book, but actually and realistically in the changing, fermenting world, that there is a people chosen to fulfill and actually fulfilling a very important world destiny, such a fact certainly cannot be ignored, and the world cannot be understood if it is ignored. You may expunge the words of a Book; it is not so easy to expunge one of the dominant facts of life. You may arbitrarily decline the idea of a Chosen Race as a Biblical proposition, but none can intelligently ignore the fact that a race is in the world actually doing all that the Bible-described Chosen Race was chosen to do. The present importance of that fact lies just here—**that race** at this moment **needs to know this** in order to extricate itself from the present distress.

For the benefit of those who have not given detailed study to this matter, let me run over some of the salient points of the evidence constituting this race. I shall have to take you back to one of your great ancestors, a man whose fame has spanned 4,000 years. When I say his name is Abraham, and that the other month we discovered his home city, Ur of the Chaldees, where he lived in houses much like our own two-storied ones, he may not seem so distant in time. Had he possessed our calendar, he could have written 1933 B. C. in his time as we write 1933 in ours. We know how he lived; we know the arts, the sciences, the financial system which were familiar to him. It was a brilliant civilization, but a brittle one, doomed to disaster because God was not in it. Wherever material progress outruns moral and spiritual progress, the knell of doom is already rung. The man Abraham is no more a myth or legend than his city or his civilization. When destructive criticism has tried its utmost solving acid formula on him, he emerges a most distinct and human personality.

Now, by some strange call, some compelling inner voice, this man was led to depart from his kindred and go out into the less settled spaces of the Semitic world, away from idolatry and materialism, to the uncontaminated silences of nature—all in obedience to a call, that certified itself to Abraham's inner consciousness as the voice of God. We shall test the validity of that in a few moments.

The simple record of it is that Abraham "obeyed and went out, not knowing whither he went." In the course of years it became clear to him in words which have come down to us, that he was to be the progenitor of a distinct people whose destiny should reach to the remotest ages. He was to become a great nation and "many nations." His descendants were to be as the sands of the sea, and as the stars of heaven. His name was to become Great. (I think we may reasonably admit that it has become great.) All nations of the earth were to be blessed through him. Father of many nations, kings and rulers were to come out of him, and his God was to be the God of his race through all the ages of time. (I think we may say also that this same God has remained the God of a certain racial stream, of which we are a part.)

Abraham had many sons, but the racial line was to

descend through one of them, named Isaac—"In Isaac shall thy seed be called." And through Isaac to Jacob, and thence through Jacob's sons—Jacob's name being changed to Israel. They were the Hebrews, which means "immigrant" or "outlander," for Abraham had been an emigrant from Ur of the Chaldees. Thenceforth they were also called Israelites, after Jacob whose name became Israel.

A Distinct People, a Divine Vehicle

In Egypt, whither these Hebrew families had gone because of famine, they became a great nation. Led out by Moses to the land that had been promised them, they organized their government and established an economic system which represents all that our Government and people are crying for today and which must become our own system ere long. And still they grew, and their destiny expanded until in King David's time it was told them by a prophet that yet one more remove awaited them—they were to be planted in another land of their own, a land they did not know, and there they would be established to be removed no more. And they became a peculiar people in the earth, separate from the nations by reason of their religion, their social code and their economic system; they were a distinct people with a distinct mission in history; through them was created this imperishable literature we call the Bible, and they were the vehicle by which was given to the world the concept of One Living God. The time came, as foretold when this nation split in two parts— one part we call the Jews. The Jews were but a comparatively small group. The others went out to fulfill their destiny, and you can identify them not only by their present fulfilling of these destinies, but by the waymarks with

which they strewed their path as they journeyed to their
appointed place. We know who the Jews are; but if we
did not know, we could identify them by means of the appointed experiences it was foretold they should undergo
amongst the nations. We may identify Israel—now
known by other names—in the self-same way.

So there can be no doubt that the idea of a Chosen
People is a basic Biblical idea. The Book declares that
"when the Most High divided to the nations their inheritance, when he separated the sons of Adam, he set the
bounds of the people according to the number of the children of Israel. For the Lord's portion is his people; Jacob
is the lot (or measuring rod) of his inheritance." Moses
declared, "The Lord thy God hath chosen thee to be a special people unto himself, apart from all people that are upon
the face of the earth." You hear that all through the
Scripture. In the Psalms and Prophets—"Israel, my
chosen," "Israel, mine elect." "You only have I known of
all the families of the earth." Of these promises Mary the
Mother of Jesus sings in the Magnificat. Our Lord Himself spoke of the "lost sheep of the House of Israel." The
Apostles Paul and Peter discuss these maters in full. They
simply cannot be disregarded by anyone who reads this
Book, whether he reveres it or not.

Of course, many people still have their own ideas
about this, and that also creates a difficulty. For when
people get their own ideas about things before they get
the facts about things, it always leads to confusion. A
man will rise and demand, "By what right does God choose
one race or people above another?" I like that form of
the question. It is much better than asking by what right
God degrades one people beneath another, although that is
implied. "God's grading is always upward. If He raises

up a nation, it is that other nations may be raised up through its ministry. If he exalts a great man, an apostle of liberty or science or faith, it is that He might raise a degraded people to a better condition. The divine selection is not a prize, a compliment paid to the man or the race —it is a burden imposed. To appoint a Chosen people is not a pandering to the racial vanity of a "superior people," it is a yoke bound upon the necks of those who are chosen for a special service. Kipling knew this when he wrote, "Take up the white man's burden."

This selection of a nation by divine choice for a special purpose has always seemed so great a thing, that men have continually asked, "Why?" And it is a great thing, and many attempts have been made to explain it. Hear Moses saying, "Ask now of the days that are past, which were before thee, since the day that God created man upon the earth, and ask from the one side of heaven unto the other, whether there hath been any such thing as this great thing is, or hath been heard like it. Did ever people hear the voice of God speaking out of the fire, as thou hast heard it, and live? Or hath God assayed to go and take him a nation from the midst of another nation, by tests, and by signs, and by wonders, and by war, and by a mighty hand and a stretched out arm? . . . " It certainly is a great thing. It was a great thing when this American nation was taken out of the midst of another great nation and made a separate constellation amongst the powers of the world. And the people asked Moses, **Why?** Moses answered it negatively: "The Lord did not choose you because ye were more in number or greater than any people (greater or better)—for ye were the smallest of all peoples; but it was because the Lord loved you and would keep the oath which he sware unto your fathers." That answer, you see, explained the continuance of the choice in after generations. It is not the complete answer for today, since Israel is now not the smallest but the greatest of the peoples. The answer for today would be: The Lord hath made you great for what He is going to make you do.

The One Idea That Has Survived

The Apostle Paul, in his Epistle to the Romans, also gives an answer to the question, **Why?** He said the Chosen people still continued chosen even in his time because "the gifts and calling of God are not subject to change"—they are absolute and unconditional. There were no "if's" in this great racial choice. It was not said, "If you obey me, you shall be my people." It was said you **are** my people and you **shall** obey me. And in that **shall** we find a key to what we are going through today. But finally, the Apostle Paul referred the choice of the people back to the sovereignty of God—"Hath not the potter power over the clay, of the same lump to make one vessel of distinction, and another vessel for ordinary use?" That is as far as written words of explanation can go. The fuller answer can only be found in the actual outworking in history of the purpose which was to be accomplished through the people so sovereignly chosen. By what right did God do this? If the right people were chosen for a right purpose, it must settle any question as to the right to make the choice. Anyone has the right to do what is right—and we certainly cannot deny this right to Deity.

So then, suppose all these promises of God were illusions of Abraham's mind; suppose they were delusions of grandeur, vain desire of distinction for his posterity—they would have died when Abraham died. Delusions die with the deluded men. They do not translate themselves into substantial and continuing realities. If these promises had been the creation of men's imagination, no matter how sincerely the men may have believed them to be the Word of God, they would have come to naught. If there was not then and there selected and predestined a servant-ruler race, then that race has not ruled or served. So it is not entirely a matter of faith; we can test it by history. Either it is valid as fact, or it is invalid as a pious dream.

Of one fact we may be perfectly certain; the **idea** of a chosen Race did not vanish with the patriarchs. It out-lived Abraham's time and his great-grandchildren's time. It reached down 400 years to Moses' time. Another 450 years and it is a living, dominant idea in King David's time. Another 300 years and we find it swaying the major Prophets, Isaiah, Jeremiah and Ezekiel. Go on 300 years, and its regal sway is just as great in the last book of the Old Testament as in the first. It lived through the 400-year gap between the Old Testament and the New, being distinctly present and potent in the Apocrypha. It ap-pears in the Gospels, Epistles and Apocalypse. It was living in the time of the Great Reformation. The common language of our Pilgrim forefathers enshrined it. The prayer book of the Episcopal church and the hymns of Christendon use its phraseology. And it has survived to be spoken and believed this November day in Dearborn in the year of Our Lord 1933. This is an amazing gen-ealogy for an idea—an expanse of 4,000 years in which **practically every idea which mankind started out with has been changed! Yet this IDEA, this BELIEF has survived.**

Some Clear Marks of Identity

Is there an outer, living, visible counterpart in history of this idea which is in the Bible? We think so because the Scriptures are full of the marks by which we may know this race. They are Religious, Social, Political and Physical marks. Note the marks and then match them with the people they fit. All of these marks are distinctly given in the Bible.

Religious marks. This Chosen race will **believe in the living God of Israel.** Take a globe of the world and mark where this faith in God is held; you will find very decisive boundary lines, defining the peoples of whom you are a part. **This race will have the Scriptures.** Amongst Anglo-Saxons and kindred peoples the Bible is the people's Book; in other nations where the Scriptures exist at all, it is the Church Book. There is a difference. Nine-tenths of the Bibles in the world come from British and American Bible Societies. This people will be found **keeping the Sabbath.** Sunday is kept in many places, but not a religious Sabbath. In European countries, elections are held on Sunday, except where this race rules. In Anglo-Saxon and kindred lands the Sabbath is a day of worship and rest, established by military, political, commercial and judicial practice. There is a vast difference between the Continental Sunday and the Anglo-Saxon Sabbath. This race is to be **a missionary race,** giving the Scriptures to the peoples of the earth. Of all the religious, medical and educational missionaries of the world, 95 per cent are sent out and supported by Great Britain and the United States. They do not preach a church-system—they disseminate the liberating Scriptures. "Cast ye up in the desert a highway for our God." Our people from of old have done that. They formed the living highway along which Christ travelled across Europe to Britain and America. St. Paul followed their trail. And they are now the highway by which Christ's Gospel goes to the islands of the sea. Our short-

comings are many, we sin in grievous ways, yet one-half
of the Sunday School attendance of the world is in these
seemingly careless United States, and most of the other
half is in other Anglo-Saxon lands. These are the religious
marks of a people who are to be compelled by divine pressure to do God's work in the world. They are the identification tags by which we may know this people.

Social Marks. This race was to receive and offer **a
harbor to the strangers,** the oppressed and the refugees of
the world. Have not the gates of Anglo-Saxon lands always been open gates of mercy? The political or religious
refugee has always fled to Britain or America. Our own
nation's doors have been open to the multitudes of the earth
until now they are closing—and that closing is a **sign that**
one movement of history is complete. As we listen to the
creaking of gigantic doors closing on one phase of history,
we listen expectantly for the majestic opening of the gates
of a new era. This Chosen People was to **abolish slavery.**
Britain did this in 1834; the United States in 1863; and
now the League of Nations, under Anglo-Saxon pressure,
is attacking slavery wherever it remains in the earth. The
economic liberation of mankind is the next step on the
agenda of the ages. Note the next social mark—This
Chosen Race was to be **addicted to drunkenness.** Of what
people is this truer than of the Anglo-Saxon in Britain and
the United States? No people has suffered from alcoholic
addiction as has the Anglo-Saxon. We are the scorn of
French, Spanish, Italian and German peoples because of
our guzzling. Even the Turk and Hindoo despise us for
it. And we are still in the throes of the alcohol problem;
we have repealed prohibition, but we have not repealed the
liquor question.

A People Searching for Itself

Political Marks. This race was to be **located North and West of Palestine,** and this is rather strange when you consider it, for Semitic peoples had a tendency to look East and South. Yet these ancient Scriptures pointed toward the cold North and the unknown West—precisely the places where we now find this race to be. They are to **have possession all round the world**—and I need not stop to remind you who are the successful colonizing people of history. They were to be **a separate people** not coalescing with the others; they swallow up peoples, but are not swallowed by them. This was Napoleon's complaint against Anglo-Saxons, and is the world's complaint today. But it was written of old that we "should dwell alone." They were to **rule the seas.** Sea-power today is entirely in Anglo-Saxon hands; the oceans are their domain. And air-power will follow in its course. They were to be **a Great People and a Company of Nations**—two branches of power foretold in Jacob's time—the one fulfilled in the American Republic, the other in the British Commonwealth of Nations. They were to hold **the desolate heritages of the earth.** They do. They were **never to be conquered by the Gentile races.** They never have been. **And they were to lose the knowledge of who they are until the latter days.** Was ever stranger spectacle seen in this world than a people searching for itself? The churches and their scholars and the historians and the archaeologists have searched and enquired and hunted for this great people of Bible prophecy which was "lost." And the Jews have been praying for the discovery of this people every Sabbath for ages. A people searching for itself! How striking is this fulfillment of a score of prophecies! But in the latter day the veil was to be removed from our eyes, and we were to discover who we are. And that, too, is coming to pass.

The Material Marks, I will not delay to mention now. They will appear when we discuss the original economic law of our race, the only successful economic system that has ever been operated on this earth. This people was to have great public wealth, and when they put into practice God's law of distribution, this public wealth was to be privately enjoyed—the present awful spectacle of a rich country full of poor people will then be a bad memory of our disobedient past. Wealth! It is the promise of God to His servant race. It is a promised part of their equipment for their covenanted work. God has fulfilled that promise. The wealth is here. When we fulfill God's economic law, as we shall have to do very soon now, that wealth will flow to every family, and then we shall be able to say as it was said in days when Israel lived under the economic law of the Lord: "I have been young, and now am old, yet have I never seen the righteous forsaken or his seed begging bread." The people who lived under God's economic law could say that.*

Here then is a bird's-eye view of race, its reason, its meaning and its marks as we spell them out in the Bible. In later talks we shall follow this race to America. We Americans must get a clear view of our place in the divine scheme of things. We must learn the chart of our destiny from the Scriptures, we must know and honor the Covenant under which we are born.

Let us free our mind of all misconceptions of this truth. Glorious as it is, inspiring us as it does with a sense of God at work today even as He worked in Bible times, it leaves no ground for human boastfulness. This is God's

*See pages 272-291, "God's Covenant Race."—Anderson.

glory, not man's. To be of the Chosen People provides no
stimulus for human pride. It bows us to the dust to know
how sadly in our ignorance and our sin we have dishon-
ored God's purpose in us. The fact of a Chosen People
is a source of solemn joy, but its implications drive us to
our knees for mercy and to the Scriptures for light.

ISRAEL AS TWO NATIONS

The Union, Division, and Final Dispersion of Israel

By W. J. Cameron, Detroit, Michigan—1933 A. D.

In our last lecture we established the fact that **the idea**
of a Chosen People is a basic Biblical idea, intrinsic in
every part of the Bible—in Chronicle and Laws, in Prophecy and Psalm, in Gospel Epistle and Apocalypse. It began with Abraham and survived all the generations of his
descendants as recorded in the Scriptures, until the Canon
of the Books was closed, thereafter surviving in the faith
and teachings of the two Biblical religions, Judaism and
Christianity. We established the fact that this character,
of a Chosen People was applied to those descendants of
Abraham who afterwards became the Nation of Israel.
Today, we are to trace as briefly and clearly as we can the
history of that Nation as it appears in the Bible, and as it
flows on out of the Bible into the stream of what we call
secular history.

Of course, I do not wholly accept the division of history into sacred and secular. We all agree that there is a
difference in the quality of the written history which these
terms describe. But the greater part of history transpired,
and is transpiring, without any written record at all, either

sacred or secular—it is all one. The living stream flows
so copiously above and beneath and around the record,
that most of it escapes. Writing history is like trying to
catch the rain in a glass-tube, you will doubtless catch
some drops, but the rain will escape you. There is a secular record of history running parallel with what we call
the sacred history of the Bible—we read it in the records
and in the monuments of the nations which we are digging
up every day—so that we are able to compare these two
types of history. And this is what we find; that as a fact,
sacred history is more reliable than secular, the reason
being that secular history, especially in the times we are
considering, was written largely for the glory of man and
shamelessly conceals many shameful facts, whereas sacred
history has no such purpose and need not diminish its facts
regarding events or individuals. Jacob was a cheater;
Moses was a murderer; David was guilty of a heinous sin;
Peter was a liar—the Bible is not concerned to conceal a
single shocking fact; it tells the truth about its heroes in a
way secular history dare not and **it can do this because
the human fact is not the history.** The true story of the
world is the story of **God working in the world,** and that is
the Bible story.

We Can No Longer Read History and Omit God, the Mind of History

The story of God's works in the structure of the earth,
we call geology; the story of God's works in the organization of living forms, we call biology. In Scripture we have
the story of God's works in the higher field of living men
and nations. Imbedded in the strata of Scripture we find
the Mind of History, the **HAND** of the Creator, as in the
ancient rocks we find "the footprints of the Creator,"

Our Bible is a small section of human history seen in a special light.   It is a very small section of the total human story—with a window let into it.   That section comprises the origin, organization and dispersion of Israel, and the coming of the Gospel—just that restricted section of the flowing human story.   And through the window of Scripture we are enabled to see God at work in history— the overtone, the underlying cause and significance, which secular history omits.   What we see there unfits us evermore to read history in the secular light.   After our vision through that window, we evermore seek God in history. And that window is the Bible.   It shows us, as Elijah showed his servant, the invisible hosts that make up the other half, the divine half, of our human story.

Now, as the pivot of this Biblical history, we have the Nation of Israel.   It is composed of 13 tribes.   They take form in Egypt—not as slaves, as some may think; our fathers never have been slaves or barbarians—but as one of the peoples of that country, distinct from all other peoples.   They revolted and emigrated from Egypt because of taxation problems—our people have always done that. There have been three major historical movements, three breakaways of Israel, and in each case the immediate occasion was taxation.   First, when Israel came out of Egypt on account of the heavy labor levies of Pharaoh.   Again when Israel seceded from Judah because of the labor tax enforced by Solomon, which Solomon's successor refused to relieve.   And the third time, when Israel of the Isles had partly settled in the American colonies, the Stamp Tax led to the great division that separated what is now the United States from Great Britain.

Emerging from Egypt and entering the land which 400 years before had been promised them, the land of

Palestine, they made it their own by right of eminent spiritual domain. I hope you will pardon my coining that expression, but there certainly is such a thing as eminent spiritual domain. Of course, everything about this matter is subject to more or less of challenge these days, and the right of Israel to the land is one of them. The promise made 400 years before its fulfillment gave a reason for the length of time that would elapse before the promise could be realized—it was said that the iniquity of the then inhabitants of the land was not yet full. A 400-year day of grace was given the original inhabitants to check the moral declension which was ruining them. But the sin and the ruin continued, and after four centuries Israel marched in. It is rather strange to think that, in our own times, which also were included in the prophetic forelook, Israel was again to have that land, and Israel does have it in the Anglo-Saxon-British people who hold a mandate they will never relinquish. There is no doubt of that. But these are detail matters, more suited to class study than a public lecture.

In the land of Palestine, Israel established a form of social life which Josephus coined a word to describe—he called it a "theocracy"—the government of God; the kingdom of God. It was a pure democracy. Democracy also is under question today, many holding that it has failed; and, in our form of it, doubtless it has not met all our hopes. But we omit one factor. What we mean by democracy, namely, the highest liberty and happiness of a people, is not an impossible ideal; our mistake has been to think it could be attained by the rule of men. It can only be attained by the government of God, which is a government of laws within a people whose highest wisdom is to permit themselves to be governed by the given laws of God.

Israel's theocracy, in this sense, represented the purest form of democratic commonwealth, or republican democracy. In fact, the inspiration of the American republic in many of its basic elements is traceable to the familiarity of our much-maligned Calvinistic forefathers with these matters. They knew much more of Israel's democracy than we do, and their knowledge was part of the uneasiness of kings in their day.

The Israel Democracy Insured The Highest Form of Social Life

Under that democracy Israel was given the laws of a noble human life upon earth. I hope you will find these laws for yourselves, in the legislation of the Bible. Laws of public order and private rights; laws of sanitation and public health—which underlie the practices of our modern health boards; laws of taxes and military service; the most enlightened land and loan laws the world has ever known; criminal laws which make our own seem silly; laws of physical safety and social welfare; laws of testimony and court procedure, which are still the bulwarks of our justice; agricultural and commercial laws; and the profoundest statements of economic law ever made, which I trust we shall study in another course—in short, all the laws which today represent the most potent civilizing influences amongst the most potent people of this planet,—these were the early equipment of Israel.

Like ourselves, these people were not content. They would experiment. They would try if human wisdom were not, after all, preferable. And so, according to the language then in use, the people went after strange gods. Now, when you read in the Scriptures that Israel went after

idols, you must not think of it as a religious desertion or a
theological revolution. It was nothing of the kind. What
attracted Israel to the idolatrous systems round about them
was the fact that the idols of the people permitted certain
economic practices which Jehovah prohibited. I am coming to that, when we take up the great economic law of
Israel. Just now I point out the fact, that the idols were
the center of economic systems which were built on price
and profit, producing riches and poverty side by side, and
that is what attracted Israel. They kept Jehovah as the
center of their religious life, but their business life was in
most particulars ruled by these other gods which were
more liberal. Very like ourselves. We wouldn't give up
the Sermon cn the Mount for anything, but at the same
time we do not think that Wall Street or Griswold Street
or LaSalle Street is any place for it! Business never likes
to mix business with religion. Just in passing, there is another remark I should like to make. There are wise individuals who say that when we speak of Jehovah, we are just
speaking of another superstitious invention of some desert
tribes; all these people invented their own gods. Yet, when
a people invents its god, the god is usually very agreeable
to what the people wish. What the god directs is what
the people desire. There is no clash. Now, there was
always a clash between Jehovah and Israel. His law was
contrary to Israel's desires. And that marks Jehovah off
from all the gods we know. It is a very important fact.

The Deep Line of Division Which The Bible Makes
Between Israel and Judah

So they became restless under the government of
God and asked for a king, like the nations about them.
You should read the story of how God spake to Samuel,

the last of the theocratic rulers, and said, 'Give them a
king, but first tell them what a king will do to them." Samuel's oration is an amazing description of human government.

Now all this time, though the nation was growing in
greatness and power, there was a deep split running
through it, a sharp line of division, which is important for
us to know, for it continues to this day. As I said, there
were 13 tribes comprising the nation, just as the Highland
and Lowland Scots, the Ulster Irish and the Southern Irish,
the Welshmen and the Cornishmen, Yorkshiremen, Lancashire men, Cockneys, Manxmen and Gurnsey men make
up the people of the British Isles—different from each
other, yet one people. Well, there was in Israel a deep
division like that which exists between the Irish and the
English. It is an important fact.

The division was between Israel and Judah. I know that
many people think that these are synonimous terms, but
they are not. All the people of Judah were Israelites, but
all the people of Israel were not Judahites. It is the same as
saying that all the citizens of Michigan are citizens of the
United States, but all the citizens of the United States are
not citizens of Michigan. In the Bible record, Judah and
Israel are distinct from the very beginning, and the distinction deepens as the record proceeds. The line between
them is as plain as day to anyone who reads the Bible with
half an eye. Hear the note of separation in Moses' prayer
when he says, "Hear, Lord, the voice of Judah, and bring
him unto his people." Hear the Psalmist say, "When Israel went out of Egypt . . . Judah was his sanctuary and
Israel his dominion." Separately mentioned, you see. The
leaders in Israel were not mainly of the Tribe of Judah,
but were largely supplied by the Joseph tribes. Moses was

not a Jew of Judah, he was of the tribe of Levi. Joshua
was of Ephraim, a Joseph tribe. Deborah was of Ephraim.
Samuel was of Ephraim. Saul, the first king, was of the
tribe of Benjamin, which hundreds of years later was to
produce the great Christian Apostle Paul. From this it is
clear that Judah was not always the leader in Israel. And
so we could go on. When Saul took his first census, the
report of it is given this way: "The children of Israel were
300,000, and the men of Judah were 30,000"—the line of
division extended even to giving them different classifica-
tions in the census reports. The same distinction was
made in King David's census, years later: "And there
were in Israel 800,000 valiant men that drew the sword;
and the men of Judah were 500,000 men." You see how
frequently they are named apart. When David was made
king after the fall of Saul, it comes out quite clearly as we
read: "And the men of Judah came, and there anointed
David king over the house of Judah"—he was king over
only one part of the nation at first. Read on: "Then came
all the tribes of Israel to David . . . and they anointed David
king over Israel. David was 30 years old when he began
to reign, and he reigned 40 years. In Hebron he reigned
over Judah seven years and six months, and in Jerusalem,
he reigned thirty and three years over all Israel **and** Judah." You see how the historians of this people always
mention the **two branches** of this people, even when they
had united under one king. It would seem that this should
have prevented our inveterate habit of confusing Israel
with Judah, and of thinking that the Jews are meant whenever we use the term Israel.

I could go on to the Prophets, and from Isaiah and
Jeremiah and Ezekiel, as well as from the Minor Prophets,
take literally scores of quotations showing how vividly

these Prophets marked the distinction, and how they expected this division and difference to exist for a long time.
But we are merely following the history now, not the
prophecy.

David the great king died; Solomon succeeded, whose
reputation for wisdom and whose brilliant reign is known
to all. But it was a prosperity that bore hard on the people. In a finanical way the times were "good," as we say,
but there is another and better kind of "good times" than
mere business and financial good times, as these people
were finding out. Solomon's fame as a ruler is dimmed
by the fact that he sowed the seeds of unrest and dissen-
sion amongst the people; his public prosperity spelt their
private poverty. And then, as to. all, death came to King
Solomon, and his son Rehoboam was about to succeed in
his stead—when something happened!

How the Anglo-Saxon-Israel People Separated from the House of Judah

Down came Israel some days before the coronation.
And Israel sent a deputation to Rehoboam with this message: "Your father made our tax burden too heavy; if
you will make it lighter we will be your loyal subjects."
Rehoboam said, "Give me three days to think it over."
And then he consulted with the elder statesmen. The old
men told him, "You do right by these people of Israel, and
they will do right by you." This counsel was not entirely
to Rehoboam's mind, so he advised with his companions,
the young bloods of his court, and they said, "Go and tell
those people that if they think your father was hard on
them, they'll find out that your little finger is thicker than
your father's loin." And that is the answer Rehoboam
made to Israel, and when he uttered it, the shout arose.

"To your tents, O Israel!" and the House of Israel separated from the House of Judah until this day.

They became two nations, and are now two distinct peoples. One part of them we call today the Anglo-Saxon, Celtic and kindred peoples, and the other part we call the Jews.

Now, if you want to follow the history of these two Nations as far as the Bible gives it, you will read most of it in the Books of the Kings and the Books of the Chronicles. Bible readers are often confused by the likeness and unlikeness of the Books of Kings and Chronicles, but like many Bible problems it yields to careful, observant reading. These books are the records of **two** nations. The Books of the Kings are mainly the records of the nation of Israel; the Books of the Chronicles are mainly the history of Judah. The two nations were related much as Canada and the United States are, only Israel, the northern nation, was greater, being comprised of ten tribes, while Judah, the southern nation, was comprised of three tribes. Israel's Book of Kings will refer to the affairs of Judah, but only briefly, and Judah's Book of Chronicles will mention the affairs of Israel with equal brevity. Take, for example, the 15th chapter of I Kings; there we have the record of three kings of Judah and their reigns compressed into 24 verses. Now if you turn to II Chronicles and read the record of those same kings you will see that it occupies 171 verses, or eight whole chapters. You read in the Chronicles how lovely was the beginning of Solomon's reign; you read in Kings how bloody it was. If you read only the Chronicles you would never know the first thing about Elijah and Elisha. There is only one brief, non-informative mention of Elijah in all of Judah's record; it says: "There came a letter from Elijah the prophet." That is

all. Yet when you turn to Israel's record in the Kings you
will find that Elijah and Elisha are headliners clear
through from the 17th chapter of I Kings to the 13th chapter of II Kings—a period of 68 years. Why? Because
Elijah and Elisha were prophets to the House of Israel
and not to the House of Judah. It is just the same thing
as United States history making very brief mention of
Canadian prime ministers, and of Canadian history making equally brief mention of United States Presidents.
They are the histories of two separate peoples and each
emphasizes its own affairs.

With that, then, I leave you to follow the remainder
of the Bible history of Israel and Judah in these two Books.
You will see how, finally, both these kingdoms came to an
end—Israel falling before the Assyrians in the year 721
B. C., and Judah being carried off to Babylon 125 years
later, in the year 586 B. C. Israel had been a separate
nation for 214 years—or nearly 60 years longer than the
United States has been a nation, and Judah retained its
nationhood for 349 years, or over twice as long as the
United States has lived thus far. The whole national
life of Israel and Judah, both united and separated, had
lasted more than 1,200 years, or twice as long as America
has been discovered. So Israel goes to Assyria, and Judah
a century and a quarter later to Babylon. The prophets
foretold what was to become of these two peoples. Israel
was to drive its way through the nations on to its appointed place in the West; Judah was to return to Palestine in
70 years. And in 70 years Judah's return was completed.
This is a fact of history.

The Foretold Movement of our People to be Settled in a Land Then Unknown

I must now take you back for a moment to the time of King David, the first great king of the United peoples of Judah and Israel under the national name of Israel. We have been speaking of the House of Judah and the House of Israel as distinct nationalities or powers. We must now make note of a third house—the House of David. You will read in the 17th chapter of the first Book of Judah's Chronicles, that the Prophet Nathan came to David and told him two things, prefacing each with the solemn "Thus saith the Lord." The first was this: "I will ordain a place for my people Israel, and will plant them, and they shall dwell in their place, and shall be moved no more; neither shall the children of wickedness waste them any more as at the beginning." A strange saying. **They had a place**—they had the land of Palestine—they were established there in peace and power. Nothing seemed less probable than that they should ever move. Yet here was a plain declaration that Israel should be moved to a place from which they should be moved no more. It may interest you to know that when Dr. Moffatt made his recent great new translation of the Bible, he was approached to see what he could do to eliminate that expression, "I will ordain," or "I will appoint." Interested people wanted him to change the note of futurity, wanted him to try if it could not be translated, "I have appointed a place," that place being Palestine. Dr. Moffat had to follow the original— it was to be **a new place,** future to David's time, another place than Palestine. If you read the still more recent translation of the Bible made by Dr. Goodspeed and the associated scholars of the University of Chicago, you will find the same result. It is there.

The second thing said to David was that his royal
house was to be established over Israel forever more—a
prophecy which raises the question, Where is the throne
of David now? That prophecy was uttered in the year
975 B. C. About 390 years later the last king of David's
line ceased to rule—**so we commonly say.** If this is true,
then one prophecy of the Bible has proved false. The
church realizes the dilemma, and to evade the consequenc-
es it adopts the expedient of spiritualizing the meaning of
this prophecy; it says that Christ was of David's line, and
that the throne of David was perpetuated in Christ's spiritual reign. If you read the prophecy, you will see that
this evasive interpretation does not meet the case.

The Author of the 89th Psalm Charges God with Breaking His Word

It would not have met the case of the man who wrote
the 89th Psalm, for example.

Here was a man whose writing is imbedded in this
sacred Book, and he regarded the prophecy as meaning
just what it said, and he felt that God's word had been
proved false. He wrote after the fall of Judah. He saw
the ruin of the royal House of David. He saw how all
the divine promises had been falsified—**seeing as far as he
could see.** And he wrote that 89th Psalm, addressing it
to God, and charging God to His face with breaking His
divine word. It is one of the most remarkably bold utterances in the Bible. It proves this Bible an honest book.

This man goes on and recites line by line every element in that promise given to David for the establishment
of his house. He quotes that prophecy uttered by Nathan
nearly four centuries before. He quotes the words of
God—"Once have I sworn by my holiness that I will not

lie unto David. His seed **shall** endure forever, and his throne as the sun before me. My covenant **will I not** break, nor alter the thing that has gone out of my lips." Thus this man lays the foundations of his case;—writing mayhap amidst the deportees of a foreign land, writing from a bitter sense of humiliation because of the downfall of Judah, he flings back at God the charge—"But thou **hast** made void the covenant of thy servant; thou **hast** profaned his crown by casting it to the ground. Thou **hast** made his glory to cease, and cast his throne down to the ground." It is the lie direct. And it is in the Bible. The Bible is an honest Book.

That man probably knows more now. At least we know more. What happened at the fall of Judah? Let us see. Zedekiah, the last king of David's race in Palestine, saw his sons and all the royal princes slain before his eyes, and then his own eyes were put out by Nebuchadnezzar, his Babylonian conqueror, and he was bound in chains and carried to Babylon and put in prison until he died. Nebuchadnezzar thought he had exterminated the seed royal. You may read it all in the stirring Book of the Prophet Jeremiah.

The Irish Harp of David, The Sweet Psalmist of Israel

But had he exterminated the royal seed? If you will read that Book of Jeremiah, you will see something else. You will see that this Prophet Jeremiah, with his secretary Baruch, by reason of a political favor, was allowed to escape to Egypt. And with him went the King's daughters. He took them to Egypt—you should read that story—and then, so far as the Bible record is concerned, silence falls. We hear no more in Holy writ of

Jeremiah or the King's daughters. That is,—**until we go
to Ireland.** There on the Four Courts at Dublin is a statue
of the Prophet Jeremiah. What earthly reason can account for a statue of the Prophet Jeremiah on the Supreme
Court of Ireland? It is like finding a statue of Ghandi on
the Supreme Court of the United States! And there is
more besides: Ireland is full of Jeremiahs. I scarcely
know an Irish family that has not one Jerry, big or little.
And though I have searched through many lists of Jewish
names, I have never found a Jew named after this great
Prophet of Judah, Jeremiah.

What does it mean? Well, they will show you in all
the ancient traditions of Ireland, that just about the time
Jeremiah and his company fade from our view in Egypt,
an old man with a secretary called Brugh, with a princess
and small company of people, appeared in Ireland to join
themselves with their people who had come over the waters from the east centuries before. And there the princess
married into the royal race of Ireland, that later spread to
Scotland, and thence to England, whose blood rules there
to this day. The old prophet gave the law on Tara Hill—
in which name some see the old Hebrew word "torah," the
Law. And the "harp that once through Tara's halls the
soul of music shed," was the same form of harp that King
David, the sweet Psalmist of Israel, played.

I would like to talk it all over with the man who wrote
the 89th Psalm. I think his heart would be as my heart
with reference to it.

But, of course, I am not making this an article of faith
for you. I only state the fact that Jeremiah and the traditions concerning him are so deeply imbedded in the ancient Irish books and in the present Celtic consciousness,
that there is no dislodging them. They are there! And to

my mind the long traditions of a people are the best of history. From Flinders Petries excavations in Egypt of the very house where Jeremiah and the princess and the little company lived—a house which has retained to our time the name of "the house of the Jew's daughter"—to the statue on the Four Courts of Dublin,—and with what we know of the sea traffic between Egypt and Ireland in ancient times,—I have a three-fold cord which I think would be gratefully laid hold upon by the sad-hearted man who wrote the 89th Psalm.

The Three Liberties Which the People of God are to Attain

But that is a digression. The House of David extinct in Judah, alive and fruitful in the Isles of the West. Read the Prophet Isaiah, as from the land of Judah he addresses Israel in the Isles. If you have a taste for Biblical criticism, you know, of course, of the great sensation which arose in the critical world a few years ago concerning the Two Isaiahs. The book of this prophecy, we were told, was written by two authors, one of them unknown, to whom was given the name of the Second Isaiah. And if you will read the book for yourself today you will see that there is a deep line of division between the 39th and 40th chapters. "Comfort ye, comfort ye, my people, saith your God"—those lines so deeply imbedded in our hearts by Handel's music. "Keep silence before me, O Islands, and let the people renew their strength. . . . Thou, Israel art my servant, Jacob whom I have chosen, the seed of Abraham my friend. Thou whom I have taken from the ends of the earth, and said unto thee, Thou art my servant; I have chosen thee, **and not cast thee away.**"—the mes-

sage to Israel in the Isles. Regarding the criticism of
Isaiah, it only concerns us to note that the deep seam, the
notable change of tone in the book, occurs just at the
point where the Prophet breaks off his view of the events
then present before him and the immediate surrounding
scene, and lifts up his eyes to **Israel in the Isles;** the glory
of that sight and the promise of future glory so lifts him
up that he pulls out all the trumpet stops of his prophetic
eloquence and unrolls the scroll of Israel's destiny to the
divinest music a prophet ever uttered.

Now, we may not seem to have made much progress
today, but really we have taken a long step forward. Our
stride has covered 1,200 years. And the reason I have
stated the various facts we have considered today, is that
they all pour into our present-day experience and
interpret our present-day situation. We have noted
that the Chosen People are two parts, one known
to itself and the world, the other "lost," as we commonly
say, but just as really present in the world and just as ac-
tively fulfilling its destiny. We shall see that this so-
called "lost people" are ourselves, "lost" only in the sense
that we have not connected our wanderings and our development and our present-day experiences with the destinies pronounced upon the people Israel of old. They
were never lost to the sight of God and His prophets. The
time foretold has come at last when Israel shall know himself and begin to do with his eyes open what he has stum-
blingly done in his blindness and his ignorance of who he
is.

The reason I am laying this racial groundwork is
that it must later serve as the foundation for what I yet
have to tell you—for I must yet tell you after this preparatory work is done, that you are a people bound under

a Law, and that you are in spiritual and economic bondage until you do it; and I must tell you that you **shall** do
this law, and that the bombardment of events will continue
to batter you until you do. For this Bible which we ex-
pound is the Constitution of Mankind's liberty. A little of
this Book entered the consciousness of our fathers, and it
became political dynamite in the world—they struck for,
they won, **political liberty.** But political liberty is a comparatively incomplete thing, it can not stand up by itself,
it never fulfills the people's pathetic hope. It requires to
be accompanied by **economic emancipation** to make it
worth its cost or to enable people to enjoy it. And much
as we prize economic liberty today, much as we desire it,
it too is an incomplete thing and will not stand by itself;
it requires for its establishment the **spiritual emancipation**
of man. These three liberties are one, the glorious liberty
of the sons of God, and all we know of them we know from
this Book in its story of our people.

That is the purpose of my work here, not a mere curious or recondite or antiquarian search for "the ten lost
tribes," certainly not our self-glorification as a superior
people. But until we know who we are, it will be difficult
to understand how this Law is bound upon our very bodies
and minds and hearts, that we as the race of Israel in all its
branches are signed and sealed and eternally sold to do
this Law, by our Creator and Sole Owner, our Father and
Redeemer, God blessed over all forever.

The Dispersion of Israel and Judah out of Their Own Land

Thus far have we come: Israel is away in the land of
the Assyrians; it is the year 721 B. C. Israel is preparing
its way to that appointed place whence it shall be moved
no more. Judah is away in Babylon; it is the year 586 B. C.

Judah is waiting the time of his foretold return to Palestine. Judah's history continues a little while in the Bible as a people that never becomes a nation again. And so we come down to the New Testament with Judah still in the land, but a vassal people. The greatest of all the Prophets, Jesus Christ, Who was infinitely more than a Prophet, though he never disdained that name, was born in the land of Judah, a political vassal of Rome. When He was born His mother Mary was on the road, making a hard journey to the place where the Roman census was to be taken; she likewise was under the rule of an alien government. And so in the New Testament we have our last Scriptural view of the Jew, and from thence he has wandered through the nations, "the tribe of the wandering foot" he calls himself, seeking a home. He has never found a home free from persecution save with his Brother Israel. Whether you say the United States, Great Britain, or modern Palestine under the British mandate, Judah can find peace only with Israel.

So we leave them today in the places whence they have been deported, one in Babylon, the other in Assyria. These were only temporary homes, however; Judah was to return to the land he left, but under alien tribute, and no more to have a king. Israel was not to return to that land, until in the latter days he should come back, as he now has come back, a conqueror. Israel was promised a world mission and a world dominion. Judah was always to know himself, his origin, his history, his descent and his name—and Judah has always known these. Israel was to be "lost," was to lose the knowledge of his very identity, until the latter days, when he was to awaken, know his name, learn his destiny, and take up his part in building the kingdom of God on earth.

From this point, in our next lecture, we can proceed. Taking our station with Israel in Assyria, we shall follow him under various names, through many lands, through all the mysteries of his lost identity, until he comes to his appointed place, renews his strength, and expands into the great peoples which the prophets foretold. And when at length we follow this people to the United States, we shall be ready to say why we came, what we are here to do, and what by our willing obedience or by the hard compulsion of events, we shall eventually do.

And in all this story we shall see the Hand of God For that is the chief romance, the greatest fact of life, the only rationale of experience—the Creating, Molding, Guarding, Guiding Hand of God.

ISRAEL'S TREK TO THE WEST

The Cipher Message—The Breakdown of Empires— Israel's Escape by the Gate—

By W. J. Cameron,
Detroit, Michigan—1933 A. D.

In our last lecture we saw the two nations, Judah and Israel, being deported to the lands of their so-called captivity—Judah to Babylon, Israel to Assyria. Their removals had been 125 years apart in time, and their new settlements were hundreds of miles apart in geographical distance. Israel, of course, went first, Judah being given a century and a quarter of grace to avoid by a cleansed national life the fate of Israel, but to no avail. And so those who had been separated into two Kingdoms in their own land were still separated in the two great empires of their captivity.

There is evidence in the Prophetic Books, however, that after Israel was taken away out of the land, an intermittent communication was maintained between the religious-minded men of both groups, that is, between Israel in Assyria and Judah yet in Palestine, for the purpose of consultation as to the meaning of events and how the prophecies uttered aforetime were to be understood with reference to the new turn of affairs. There was communication also between the deported groups and those left in the homeland, for the deportations were not **en bloc** and did not occur at one time. Later, when the deportation of Judah began, there was communication between the deported of Israel in Assyria and those of Judah in Babylon.

Now, the Prophet Ezekiel was one of those who went to Babylon with the earlier Judah deportees, and in the 14th chapter of his book he tells us that while he was sitting amongst his deported brethren in Babylon, he was visited by certain elders who came down from the Israel deportees in Assyria. Israel, a hundred years in an alien land, had no prophets, but knew that God spake in Judah as before. So these men of Israel sought Ezekiel, this Prophet of Judah. And not only did Ezekiel consult with them, he also received a prophetic message which he was commissioned to deliver to them. It is interesting and important to know this message, one of the last to be uttered directly to Israel. The address is clear—it is sent to Israel, and in terms which Israel, and no Babylonian spy, would understand: "Son of man, put forth a riddle and speak a parable unto the house of Israel"—the news was to be conveyed under the divine cipher. Read it all in the 17th of Ezekiel.

The Message Which the Prophet Conveyed to Israel Under the Divine Cipher

He tells how the conqueror sought to remove the royal seed from Judah—"a great eagle with great wings came unto Lebanon and took the highest branch of the cedar" (that is, the royal branch): "he cropped off the top of his young twigs" (that is, the younger royalty) "and carried it into a land of traffic; he set it in a city of merchants." Thus Ezekiel tells of one incursion on the land. And then he tells of a second incursion. After that comes the heart of his message to the elders of Israel. The invading kings thought they had won control for all time of the royal seed of Israel. But "Thus saith the Lord God: I too will take the highest branch of the high cedar" (the royal house) "and will set it" (I will set it, and **not** those eagle kings); "I will crop off from the top of his young twigs" (the royal children) "a tender one" (that is, a young daughter) "and will plant it upon a high and commanding mountain—(that is, the royal daughter will be made part of some high ruling house). "In the mountain of the height of Israel will I plant it" (that is, in an Israel royalty ruling somewhere in the earth, but certainly nowhere near the place where Ezekiel and his auditors were) "and it shall bring forth boughs and bear fruit, and be a goodly cedar; and under it shall dwell all fowl of every wing" (it will rule over many different peoples); "in the shadow of the branches thereof they shall dwell. And all the trees of the field (the other ruling houses and peoples) shall know that I **the Lord** have spoken and have done it."

That is the way Ezekiel made it known to the elders of Israel, who had come down from their Assyrian captivity to consult him, that Jeremiah was escaping with the

King's daughters, as we saw in our last lecture, and was fleeing with them to the Isles of the West whither many of their people had preceded them centuries before. So Ezekiel, though in Babylon, knew what was happening away to the west at the downfall of Jerusalem, and the men of Israel understood from his riddle exactly what had happened, and made their plans accordingly. But read it for yourself.

We have still another instance of communication between the parts of Judah, the one deported to Babylon and the other still remaining in Palestine; it is a letter from Jeremiah. You will find it in the 29th chapter of his book. Jeremiah was still in Palestine, and he writes to his deported brethren: "Now that you are in Babylon, be not deceived by false diviners and seers who will tell you this and that about the probabilities of your early return. For thus saith the Lord, after 70 years be accomplished at Babylon, I will visit you and perform my good word toward you, in causing you to return to this place. Therefore, settle down for a long stay, build your houses, plant your gardens, marry and raise families, and seek the peace of whatever city you have been carried to, and pray unto the Lord for it; for in the peace thereof shall ye have peace." Excellent advice. It is just such advice as we should give if the people of Wayne County were to be exiled to Mexico for 70 years—that is, until the year 2003 —settle down and make the best of it until the expiration of the term.

Now, note two things in what I have just said: first, there was communication between all the parties, between Israel and Judah in their separate exiles, as well as between the two parts of Judah at exile and at home. Second, note that the directions communicated to the two peoples, Israel

and Judah, are quite different. Judah is promised a home-
coming in 70 years. Israel is not promised that. Instead,
Israel is told of the tender royal twig cropped from the
royal house and carried away, not by conquering kings,
but by hands divinely directed. The messages to Judah
and Israel differ materially from each other.

We are not without knowledge how these deported
nations were treated in their exile. You may see from
Jeremiah's letter that these people were carrying on life
just about as they had done before, but in a strange land.
Fortunately we have two extended pictures of exile life,
if you should care to read them. If you would like to
see how Judah fared in Exile, read the Book of Esther as
it is found in our common Bible. If you would see how
Israel fared in exile, read the Book of Tobit in the Apocrypha. If you have not read Tobit you have missed a
most delightful tale. I wish everyone had a copy of the
Apocrypha; I regret it is no longer printed between the
Old and New Testaments as in the older Bibles.

A Spirit of Turmoil Shudders Through the Empires That Hold Israel

In Tobit we have the story of a very interesting deported Israel family who lived near Ninevah and did very
well for itself, both socially and financially. We learn
from it a great deal of how life went with the tribes of
Israel in alien Assyria. It matters little that Tobit is not
an historic or prophetic book—it gives a transcript of Israel's life in that foreign land just as a novel of Sir Walter
Scott pictures the life of Scotland, or an early novel of
Booth Tarkington pictures Indiana politics. They are not
historical but they are true. In this respect Tobit is a
genuine source book. And if you read it, as I hope you

will for its own quaint charm, you will observe toward the
end of the book old Tobit's anxiety for the things he felt
were coming upon Assyria. He warns his son Tobias to
take his family and flee to Media, where, as the Bible tells
us, some of the tribes of Israel had been settled. Now
Media was to the north, in the uplands of Assyria, and was
more easily defensible from military attack. Tobit had
earlier entrusted a sum of money in that part of the country. There were rumors of attack upon Assyria from outside, there were signs of revolt inside, and as we now read
the actual history of what occurred, we can see how wise
was the advice of Tobit that Tobias flee to Media. And
that such advice could be given in such a book indicates
that this was the course taken by many an Israelite family
when the affairs of Assyria became troubled. In fact,
Media was one of the gathering places whence Israel made
its break out of exile.

I trust these sidelights may help a little toward making a picture in your minds of the general situation at this
time. Two great empires have swallowed up Judah and
Israel—Judah is in the grip of the Babylonian empire to
the south; Israel is in the grip of the Assyrian empire to
the north.

And now a great drama of what we call secular history opens. The Babylonian Empire attacks Assyria: the
empire that holds Judah attacks the empire that holds Israel. It is the time of inner turmoil which old Tobit foresaw, when Assyria trembled from war without and unrest within. It is a time when the whole world seems to
be astir. Nearly a thousand years before, a similar spirit
of awakening had shuddered through the Semitic peoples
of lower Mesopotamia, and set them moving. One group
was led by Terah out of Ur of the Chaldees up toward
Canaan—a directly northwest line—and in that group

Abraham marched; it was from that group that Abraham was commanded to depart to a land that was to be shown him. At the same time another great body of people moved from the shores of the Persian Gulf to the shores of the Mediterranean—those were the Phonecians of later history. A third and perhaps larger body followed the course of the Tigris northward, and these became the founders of Asshur (named from their god) and of the Assyrian Empire.

The Road is Open for Israel to Escape—to the North and West

And now after a thousand years the world seemed in flux again. There were great stirrings amongst the people. National ambitions became strong. The desire to be on the wing, to explore, to subjugate, was regnant everywhere. After a thousand years Dedan and Sheba and Shimar and Babel and Ninévah and Media and Parthia, all the old cradle lands of our history, were again being waked into action. The Scythians were attacking Assyria from the northwest along the borders of Media. Babylon was attacking from the southeast against Nineveh, the capital of Assyria. When Scythian and Babylonian met in Assyrian territory and the war drew south again, **the door was open for Israel to pass out of Assyria if they wished.** It was a case of the officers fighting amongst themselves, leaving the prisoners free to walk away. That, however, was not the case with Judah, down south in Babylon. Judah had no door of escape but was still hemmed in; Judah had no need to escape, she knew that her future was settled for her. But Israel knew that the tender twig of the high cedar had been carried away to be plant-

ed in an Israel royal house far to the west, and Israel's
thoughts turned thither.

These, then, were the movements of secular history,
as we say. But the Prophets had seen it long before, the
remaining Prophets were seeing it now as one of the
climaxes of sacred history. Isaiah had foretold what was
going to happen to Assyria. Read it in the 10th chapter
of his book, where God speaks to Assyria—"O Assyrian,
the rod of mine anger, whose military power is the staff of
mine indigation. I will send him against an hypocritical
nation, that they may in their trouble be led back to Me.
But Assyria does not know he is but MY instrument, for
he saith, 'by the strength of **my hand** I have done it, and
by **my wisdom.'** Shall the ax boast itself against him that
heweth therewith? Shall the rod shake him that lifteth it?
Wherefore, it shall come to pass, that when the Lord has
performed His whole work against Israel, then will I turn
and punish the boastfulness of the king of Assyria, and
the glory of his high looks." That was what was transpiring now—Babylon was raised up as the rod of God's
anger against Assyria, and in its turn Babylon itself was to
suffer disaster for the same kind of ungodly pride. And
thus the Prophets saw the succession of the empires. As
we said in the last lecture, secular history is sacred history.
The human story is the story of God at work—history is
His Story.

And now in this time of turmoil, what was Israel doing? Israel could not return to their own land of Samaria, for two reasons; first, the road thither lay southwest
and the Babylonian armies blocked the way. Second,
during the 100 years they had been absent from their land,
Assyria had populated it with another people—Arabs,
Babylonians, Persians and people from Susiana. You

will remember how when Judah eventually returned to Palestine, with what scorn they regarded these mixed people of Samaria, and you will remember how in our Lord's time the Samaritans would not allow Him to rest in their towns because He was on His way to Jerusalem; and how His disciples were surprised to find him in conversation with a Samaritan woman; and how our Lord offended his people by the Parable of the Good Samaritan, when no one would allow there was such a thing; and how the deepest insult they could hurl at our Lord was, "Thou art a Samaritan." All this flowed from the difference which was felt to exist between the true people of Israel, of which Judah was now the sole remaining representative in the land, and the alien mixed people with whom the conquerors repopulated Samaria, the former land of the ten-tribed Kingdom of Israel.

So Israel had no inducement to go back to their own land. To the west, the Egyptian armies had come up; there was no escape toward the Mediterranean Coast. To the east lay the Persian and Parthian powers. Only the road north and northwest lay open. The crux of our inquiry is this: **Did Israel go out by that road?**

Micah, the Breathless Broadcaster, Describes the Great New Exodus of Israel

Now, I read my Bible, and I trace in the old maps and in the ancient historians the answer that Israel did so go out. Anyone who imagines that our contention here is entirely an extra-Biblical one, is mistaken. It is because the Bible tells us what was to occur and what was occurring, that we consider the possibility of confirmatory signs of it elsewhere. And it is because history observes a very mysterious people moving slowly across Europe, whose

origin no one seems able to account for, that we are glad
of the light the Bible may throw upon the problem.

Take the Prophet Micah. He announces what is
happening almost as a modern broadcaster would an-
nounce it (see his second chapter). With breathless sentences he describes the great scene that is hidden from the
sight of his hearers, but is fully open to the eyes of his
divinely enlightened mind—"The breaker has come up
before them!—they have broken up!—they have passed
through the gate!—they are gone out!—and their king
shall pass before them, and the Lord at the head of them!"

What a picture of what was occurring: the Babylonian and Scythian breakers coming up against Assyria and
breaking it up; Israel espying the gate left open and escaping by it; their royal house having passed on before them
by another way; and their whole movement herein directed by the purpose of God.

If you wish this in more precise words, turn to the
Apocrypha again, to the 13th chapter of Second Esdras,
and read this: "Those are the ten tribes, which were carried away prisoners out of their own land in the time of
Osea, the King, whom Shalmaneser the king of Assyria
led away captive, and he carried them over the waters, and
so they came into another land. But they took this counsel amongst themselves, that they would leave the multitude of the heathen, and go forth into a further country,
where never mankind dwelt, that they might there keep
their statutes, which they never kept in their own land.
And they entered into Euphrates by the narrow passages
of the river. For through that country there was a great
way to go, namely, of a year and a half; and the same
region is called Arsareth." If Arsareth can be identified
as in the region of the River Sereth, then Israel had made
its way to the west side of the Black Sea. In any case,

we have here a strong tradition of what became of the
ten tribes.   The route that Israel would have taken was
not an impossible one; two centuries later Zenophon led
the retreat of the Ten Thousand in the same general di-
rection of Israel's escape across the upper reaches of the
Euphrates.   In fact, Zenophon, like Israel, as Esdras tells
us, found the waters at those upper parts easy to cross.

Now hear the Chorus of the Prophets as they speak
of these events.   "Israel is swallowed up;" cries Hosea,
"now they shall be among the Gentiles as a vessel wherein
is no pleasure.   Yet the number of the children of Israel
shall be as the sand of the sea which cannot be measured
nor numbered."   "I will sift the house of Israel among
all the nations, like as corn is sifted in a sieve, yet shall not
the least grain fall to the ground," is the divine word
through Amos.   "Go ye forth of Babylon," cries Isaiah,
"flee ye from the Chaldeans, with a voice of singing declare ye, utter it even to the end of the earth; say ye, the
Lord hath redeemed his servant, Jacob."   And Jeremiah
cries, "Hear the word of the Lord, O ye nations, and declare it in the Isles afar off and say, he that scattered Israel
will gather him, and keep him as a shepherd doth his flock."
All of these utterances indicate a knowledge of what was
transpiring with regard to Israel, and what the end of it
would be—arrival, reorganization, renewal of strength
and the rediscovery of their God in the Isles.   Indeed, Jeremiah is so moved by the mighty character of these events
that he asserts twice in his prophecy that it means **an entirely new beginning in the history of Israel,** and in the
way men speak of history.   Up to this time the great event
in Israel's history and the world's was the emergence
of Israel from Egypt.   "But the days come, saith the Lord,
when men shall no more say, By the life of God who
brought Israel up from the land of Egypt, but, By the

life of God who brought Israel up, and conducted the race of the house of Israel from the land of the North." A new order of things in the world, so great as to supersede the memory of former great things. Oh, the prophets knew!

But to return to the lower order of facts which have more weight with this generation. What is our factual ground thus far, We **know** that Israel was deported to Assyria in two or three bodies and settled in two places, one in northern Mesopotamia and the other in Media. We **know** that while Israel was in those parts of Assyria, the Assyrian Empire broke up. We **know** that only one way lay open if Israel wished to escape during the confusion. We **know** that the Prophet Micah said that they had escaped. We **know** that Ezekiel had given Israel intimation of where the royal house was to be planted again. We **know** that the Apocryphal book of Second Esdras records the definite tradition that Israel or a part of Israel had gone up to the Caucasus in the region of the Black Sea, which we **know** was not an impossible route for it was followed two hundred years later by other men.

The Pivotal Fact: Israel's New Name as Found on the Monuments

And we know one more fact, a valuable one; we **know** the name which Israel bore in Assyria. They were not called Israel; they were called **Khumri.** If you recall what the prophets say about Israel losing its name and being known by other names, this will not surprise you, but the confirmation of this is not in the Bible, it is in the sculptured records of Assyria. How did Israel come to be called **Khumri?** The sixth king of the separated kingdom of Israel was named **Omri.** We know little of him directly except that he built Israel's capital city of Samaria, so that often the kingdom of Israel was spoken of as Samaria, just as we sometimes refer to the United States Government as Washington. But this man apparently did have a considerable reputation outside of the Bible. He was evidently an internationalist and was well known in the kingdoms and empires round about. From a certain denunciation uttered by the Prophet Micah we gather that he changed the whole economic law of Israel, and we know that he made a treaty with Tyre, the great commercial nation. He was a king who sold the Economic Law of the Lord for the quicker profits of Tyre. And so we find a strange thing connected with his name, a very unusual thing in the Bible, for though in the Book we hear much of the Law of the Lord and the Statutes of Israel, to name laws or systems by **men's** names is most unusual. I recall only one instance, and that was in the case of King David,—until we come to King Omri. One of the bitter things said about Israel in the days of its downfall was that it kept "the statutes of Omri." Moses laws and statutes were designed to erect in Israel a godly economic system that would make imperfect and unjust human economic systems obsolete, and no king who followed them would have gained much international fame. But so widely known was Omri that Assyria ever after called the Kingdom of Israel, **the House of Omri,** or "**Beth Khumri.**" It is so written on the Assyrian monuments of the reign of Shalmaneser and exists to this day. **The Khumri were the Israelites of the captivity.**

Now the importance of this to us lies just here— whereas we could find little or no trace of the so-called Lost Ten Tribes of Israel under their own name, we find many traces of the **Khumri** in the ancient records. We find their name first in the parts of Assyria where Israel

was settled. We find it afterward across that narrow
neck of water which separates the Sea of Azof from the
Black Sea, that is, in the country we now know as the
Crimea. It requires no great gift to see the family resem-
blance between "Khumri" and "Crimea." Two hundred
years later we find the Khumri, now called Kymbri, far up
the Danube, in what we know as Bavaria. And there they
are met by another column of Israel escaped out of Assyria by the east coast of the Caspian Sea, who after many
years made a junction with the Kymbri host, and this second column bore several names on its long slow trek.
They were called the Sacae and the Massagetae and the
Getae and the Goths and finally the Saxons (spelled several different ways) under which names of Goths and
Saxons they were known for centuries. Those who went
north to Scandinavia returned in part as the Normans.
Those who went to northern France became known as
Britanni. Those who went southwest to Spain, Celtiber-
ians. Those who went to what is now Holland retained
the name of Sacsons. Those who went up to Denmark
were called Jutes. The last place we find the name Kymri
is in the present land of Wales. They are the Cimbric
people of the present day. All of these lines, Dane and
Norman, Saxon and Angle converged on what are now
the British Isles, and there built a new empire—which is
now the one remaining large empire in the world. They
were originally the People Israel. In this swift glance at
the process, I do not prove each step, I only seek to show
you the bridge across which we walk. We have the indisputable starting point with the Khumri, and with that
key and a student's patience, the successive steps of the
history are easily worked out for yourselves.

Our Names, Our Waymarks, and Our Historic Sea-ways and Highways

But that is not the whole story by any means. While this escape from Assyria has occupied us, other matters were transpiring in the world. We must not forget that for centuries there had been great traffic along the Mediterranean to the Sicily Isles, off Land's End, England, and to the tin mines of Cornwall. The merchants of Tyre, the great Phenician traders, had regular routes through the Strait of Gibraltar, known to the ancients as the Pillars of Hercules, up to the Isles of Britain. If you read the book of Jonah you will see that it was quite the usual thing for a man to go down to the seaport at Joppa and pay his fare to Tarshish. Now Tarshish was in Spain, west of the Strait of Gibraltar, facing the Atlantic, and the grave of one of the tribute or tax-collectors of King Solomon has been found there. We read of Solomon's navy which went to West Africa. We hear of the maritime tribe of Israel, the tribe of Dan, whose ships are often mentioned in the Old Testament, and we find Dan's habit of leaving his name in all the places he visited, and we think it can be traced in the Rivers Danube and Dneiper and in Dardana and in Danmark and in the Dannaans, the early inhabitants of Ireland. Traffic in those days was much greater than we commonly suppose. "The Ships of Tarshish" so often mentioned in the Old Testament, were the great ships which sailed through Gibraltar into the Atlantic to Tarshish which was situated on the southwest coast of Spain. And so all along the northern coast of the Mediterranean we find the marks of Israel settlements. And save for parts of the overland routes taken by those who escaped from Assyria, all of the other routes of Israel are perfectly clear.

If you take a map of Europe and Western Asia and
in imagination take your stand on the coasts of Israel, you
will see where the lines ran.   You look straight up the
Adriatic to Germany and Holland and Britain.   Or you
look straight up through the Boot of Italy to the same
countries.   And if you miss these invitations of geographical indentations and the inclinations of coastlines, and sail
out through Gibraltar, you hug the coast until you come to
the Isles of the West.   And everywhere you will find the
names, the traditions, the institutions of this people Israel.
You will find the name Iberia between the Caspian and
the Black Seas—you will find it later denoting the land
we know as Spain—and a little later denoting Hibernia,
or Ireland.   Just as you will find the name Scot first
given to the Irish and then to the people of Scotland.   But
even before that you will find the name "Scot" in Egypt
and Greece.

Being of Scottish descent, that interests me, naturally.
The poetic name of Scotland is Caledonia, that was its
real name of old, but I find the name Caledonia first a
little west of the Black Sea on one of the early routes of
Israel to the west, long before the time of the Assyrian deportations.   For we must remember that as trouble mount-
ed on trouble, the people of Israel did not wait until the
final blow—they were moving out in some instances centuries before.   Now all the Scots are Gaels, and that name
is a perfect derivative from Galilee, the home of Israel,
and so runs to Scotland.   Straight north of Galilee I find
under the south coast of the Black Sea the name Galatia.
I find it again at the northwest tip of Portugal.   I find it
again in the name of Gaul, for France, and in the name of
Gael, for the people of Scotland.   It is therefore no wonder to me as it is to many of the scholars who write books

on "Spanish Influence in Scottish History" and similar
subjects.   One of my own family's old Scottish names is
a name whose origin can only be traced to Spain.   And
when I read another scholar's book entitled, "The Scot
in Poland," I do not wonder; it explains to me a great
deal about Poland—our people came that way.   And
when I read in history that the French kings had Scottish
regiments for their body guards, I do not wonder—they
were both Gaels.   And when I read Paul's Epistle to the
Galatians, and see what he is driving at there, I recognize
so many things about my people that I cannot help thinking of it as Paul's Epistle to the Scots in the East.   Israel,
as I have explained before, has left pockets of people, racial
influences, rearguards of liberty, all along the march.

The Spartans Were of Israel: How Ireland Signalled Ezekiel's Cipher

My friends, this Bible, God's purpose as expressed
in this Bible, the outworkings of that purpose as detailed in
the Prophets, the traces of that purpose in history—these
stretch out and touch every land.   And yet it is seemingly
impossible for some to realize that the Bible is only the
roadmap and **the actual roads run outside the Bible** in this
world of men.   It seems impossible for some to see God
outside the Book and see God's people still living and pur-
suing their course in these latter days as they did—outside the Book—in the former days.

If I were to connect ancient Greece with Israel, some
of you would probably think it mere gratuitous zeal for a
theory.   And yet there is evidence that the Spartans were
Israelites!   Their land, Lacedemon, called also Laconi,
from which we get the word "laconic" for short and sharp
speech, the proverbial speech of Israel, and themselves

called of old Lacedemonians, are directly connected with
Israel by two letters found in the first Book of the Maccabees. When the Jews under the Maccabees sent to ask
the protection of Rome, their Embassy called at Greece
with letters to the Lacedemonians. And this is what the
high priest wrote to those Grecians: "There were letters
sent in times past unto Onias the high priest, from Darius,
who reigned then among you, to signify that ye are our
brethren"—and he enclosed a copy of that earlier letter,
which reads: "Areus, king of the Lacedemonians, to Onias
the high priest, greetings: it is found in writing, that the
Lacedemonians and the Jews are brethren, and that they
are of the stock of Abraham: now therefor, since this is
come to our knowledge, ye shall do well to write to us of
your prosperity. We do write back again to you, that
your cattle and gods are ours, and ours are yours." And
so on. In reply to the letter and its enclosure, the Lacedemonians of this later time again acknowledged their
racial unity. The Spartans were Israelites. That fully
explains why they stand out in Grecian history as Israel
stood out in the history of Semitic countries.

You see we have had a large canvas in this lecture.
If we had regular class hours for a school year, and would
apply ourselves to all the sources of this knowledge, you
would see that the historical work that has been done in
this section of the subject is very complete. In what we
are doing now I can only give you a suggestion of the
method, a suggestion of the vast movement of peoples in-
volved, a suggestion of the bridge of history across which
our minds travel to this knowledge of ourselves and kindred peoples as descendants of those very people who
went forth into the world bearing their Biblical destinies
on their shoulders. They converged on the Isles as foretold. Everything of basic character they brought there

with them, their courage, their customs, their spiritual
aptitude, their undeviating progress until they reached
the appointed place, marks them out as Israel. Had you
been in the Isles in that early day you would have read in
their ships that they knew who they were—you would
have known that Jeremiah had arrived and that Ezekiel's
riddle had been readily understood, for there on the top-
most mast of every ship was the "craunnog," or tree tufts,
the tender young twigs of the highest branch of the high
trees. Up there in the strong northwestern angle of the
earth, the Danaana of Ireland and the Danes of Denmark
knew no dishonor on the seas more humiliating than to
lose the leafy cluster from the topmast. There are the
Iberians, the Hibernians, the Ga-els, which means "sons
of God." Ezekiel's parable translated in the Isles of
the West! Jeremiah in Ireland on his divine mission "to
build and to plant." And the tribes of the Captivity still
laboring slowly across Europe!

With Joseph and Jesus Among the Tin Mines of Cornwall: The Poet Blake

How long did it take them to make the journey?
Those who traveled overland, the main body of the captivity, were more than a thousand years reaching Central
Europe and Europe's western front. Remember, they did
not travel as an army with its own supplies, but as a people who had to live by the way, and whose progress was a
series of alternate settlings down and movings on again.
They did not live by war and rapine, but by their labor.
It was a long road to travel, a long road of discipline, but
that Star of the West in their traditions never set for
them. And even when they had reached the Isles, it did
not set—it led out a part of them across the Atlantic, to
America.

But when the body of Israel had penetrated as far as Central Europe, and while Israel in the Isles was attaining strength and civilized government and a strong educational system, an Event had transpired in Palestine which dwarfed all the others—the Christ was born. The little town of Bethlehem had given earth the Man who redeemed the Earth back to the divine purpose for it. Jesus was a travelled man, that much is true beyond all tradition. The Gospels make very little of that—they dispose in a few scant words even of His journey into Phenicia. Men are busy today with speculations as to where He spent the days between His boyhood and the age of thirty. They say He learned His mysticism in the East—which would be of absorbing interest if there were anything Eastern about His mysticism. There is a strong tradition that his uncle was in the tin trade with Cornwall, and indeed the Cornish miners sing a song to the effect that **"Joseph was a tin merchant."** There is a tradition that Jesus as the ward of His uncle made journeys to the Britannic Isles, or the Tin Islands, as they were called, and was even at school there in some of the colleges established centuries before by the Prophet Jeremiah. We know that Jesus' learning astonished the scholars of His day and they wondered at His education, saying "Where hath this man letters, never having been at school?" Who can say that Jesus was not at school? It is not necessary to invent miracles to account for His education. Say what you will about it all, hold what opinion you may about the tradition, you will yet account it a notable fact that in the year 1933 King George the Fifth with his assembled people stood, as they have stood together many times in former years, singing this hymn of the old Poet Blake. Hear it, and say why the tradition has lived?—

"And did those feet in ancient times
  Walk upon England's mountains green?
And was the holy Lamb of God
  On England's pleasant pastures seen?
And did the Countenance Divine
  Shine forth upon our clouded hills?
And was Jerusalem builded here
  Among these dark Satanic mills?"

I think anyone will say that this is indeed a most re-markable thing, King and Commons singing **of a time when Christ was in England!** But it is not all conjecture and tradition. The way to the Isles was a well-travelled one when Christ was born. There were men in Palestine and Egypt and Greece and Rome who knew the coasts of Ireland as they knew their homelands—you see that clearly in the Roman historians.

And so we are not at all surprised when we see two things occur: First, when the first persecution came upon the new-born Christian-church at Jerusalem, it vanished from the country, none being left except the Apostles. Where did the Church go? It went to the Isles. Christianity was planted where Israel was planted, in the west. The Glastonbury tradition seems to be a sound one. The contention that Britain was not evangelized until Pope Gregory sent St. Austin to Kent in 597 A. D. lacks historical confirmation. It is indeed a fact that the benevolent Gregory did send Austin but when Austin came and proclaimed his mission, he was met with brotherly Christian hospitality by the representatives of the Bishopric of London which had then been in existence 500 years. Within ten years of the Crucifixion, Christianity was in the Isles, forced there by persecution and arriving there over the familiar routes that Israel had used for a thousand years.

The second thing to occur was this: when the Christian Apostles began to evangelize the world, the greatest of them, the Apostle Paul, followed the coastland route of Israel and planted his churches amongst the Israel colonies along the north shore of the Mediterranean. The records of the early councils of the Catholic church are our authority for saying that St. Paul traveled as far west as the Britannic Isles, as the church records name them. If you will read Morgan's entrancing history, "St. Paul in Britain," you will see the documented evidence clearly laid out for your appraisal. It is not an astonishing thing at all, for we had always known from our Bible, from St. Paul's Epistle to the Romans, that Spain was within the boundaries of his evangelistic vision. Paul intimates in that Epistle that he had not yet visited Rome, and more than indicates that he **had** visited Spain. "Whensoever I take my journey into Spain I will come to you," he writes in Chapter 15. And again, explaining that he has to go down to Jerusalem first, he says, 'When, therefore, I have performed this, I will come by you on my way to Spain." And if to Spain why not around the corner into Britain, as the early church councils declare And if St. Paul goes to Spain at that early day, why not also Joseph of Arimathea, reputed tin merchant and uncle of Jesus, at a slightly earlier day. And if Joseph, why not also the young Jesus who knew the destiny of Israel. Anyway the fact is incontestable—Christianity on its expansion in the world followed the same course as Israel did, to the westward. Of all Paul's churches, to whom he wrote the Epistles, not one remains, and yet Paul's churches are everywhere westward in the world. It is wonderful to think of the preparatory grace of God in all these great racial movements. It is wonderful to think that our supposedly prosaic life is really part of the epic movement of God's forestated purpose.

Thus, with a shuttle of so many threads the ancient East and our own West are linked in every possible way. Prophecy shot its illumined arrows from East to West. By sea routes and coastal ports and overland roads the Chosen People travelled East to West. Our religion came from East to West. It is in the West we are at the present moment in this study. But do not suppose God's movement to be completed there. We are to see arise in the West that which is to sweep East again to bring the new world change that is coming.

So, in our next lecture we shall see the people renew their strength in the Isles, and then expand to their fortold power in the Western continent of America.

ISRAEL ARRIVES IN AMERICA
From The Isles To Plymouth Rock

By W. J. Cameron, Detroit, Michigan—1933 A. D.

In our previous lecture we saw by what stages and under what names the major part of the House of Israel made their way from Assyria through Europe. The tribes which 1,000 years before Christ had concentrated on the Western Front of Asia, we saw 1,000 years after Christ concentrating on the Western Front of Europe. It is rather strange to think that in our own times, in the Great War, Israel again stood on both these Western Fronts, but this time as united nations and great military powers.

We have seen how practically all of the time of Israel's settlement in Palestine there had been a considerable leakage of Israel's population toward the Isles of the

West. Detachments of the people had been going to and fro between Palestine and Britain for centuries, many of them settling in the Isles. But about a thousand years ago, when the last detachments came overland, under the names of Normans, Angles, Saxons, Jutes and Danes, these unrecognized tribes of the captivity were compelled to fight their several ways into the appointed place—and they all got in; not one of them could be kept out. Historians may write about the Norman Conquest, but students of the Scripture know that the Normans were but a long separated part of Israel blindly demanding entrance to the appointed place—and getting it; neither conquering nor being conquered, but reuniting and contributing their elements to the national character. Led by a destiny they could not evade, which forbade them settling in the inviting parts of Europe that fell to their lot, they were at last led into the Isles.

That is always the word to use with regard to Israel —they were 'led"—it is the word the Scriptures use. Now the word usually used of Judah is "driven," which describes a different sort of moving influence than that which "led" Israel. Israel was "led" out of Egypt, not driven. Israel was "led" out of Samaria, not driven. Israel was "led" out of Assyria, not driven. Israel was "led" across Europe, not driven. Israel was "led" into the Isles, not driven. And Israel was "led" into America, not driven hither. That leading for Israel still exists, and Israel can go as fast and as far as it follows the leading. Today, Israel is not submitting to be led, and thus our spiritual and economic captivities still linger upon us. The geographical leading has been accomplished in its westward movement. Israel itself shall be no more moved out. But by the judgment of God certain alien systems and cus-

toms will be moved out of Israel—we are seeing the beginning of that now. The geographical movement is now
superseded by the spiritual movement.

This is Not a Doctrine That Exalts Any Race or Nation, But the Power of God

When the tribes and parts of tribes which went to
the Isles by the sea routes centuries before, were invaded
by the tribes which came slowly overland across Europe
centuries later, the ruling prophetic word was, "Keep
silence before me, O Islands, and let the people renew
their strength." In the Islands Israel did renew its strength
in every way—strength of law and national unity, and
racial power; strength of population, religion and wealth.
And from England, Israel began to realize its inheritance
of the earth. They won control of the seas in great ac-
tions which, had they been written in the Old Testament,
when men more clearly saw God's hand in events, would
surely have been given a miraculous content. They spread
into many lands. Their language became the highway
of the world's thought and poetry and religion.

We who teach this truth concerning Israel, are sometimes accused not only of being self-glorifiers, but also of
being definitely pro-British in emphasizing the gathering
of Israel in the Isles. I once heard a minister say, "Oh,
what you say is just English egotism—the English always
think themselves better than anyone else." It is a defect
which I have observed is not confined to the English. But
as for this being an English doctrine, let me say that it is
as much rejected by Britons as by Americans. As a matter of fact, this doctrine originated in Palestine, in the
Bible, and if Britain controls Palestine today and if America finances Palestine, it is only because the Prophets fore-

told that in the latter days Israel would do these things.
Whenever you find a people doing what Israel was to do,
you have discovered the Identity.   Whether we as a
people accept or reject the truth that we are Israel, the
fact is that on broad lines we are fulfilling it. That part
of the plan which depends upon God's given word goes
steadily forward.   This people foretold and predescribed
is here.

In other terms than I use here, men and women are
always recognizing this. A preeminent fact in the world
diplomacy today is the unity of the Anglo-Saxon people
which promises to supersede the League of Nations. That
unity was long ago foretold.   We of the United States
did not create that unity, indeed we have raised every
barrier against it.   We have made war twice on England,
and threatened war several times. We have spread anti-
English prejudice through our school books for 150 years.
We have allowed our country to be used as a base for
virulent anti-British propaganda.   And yet Anglo-Saxon
unity stole upon the world as irresistibly as the Springtime
comes.   One of the phrases coming to the fore today is
"the English-speaking peoples."   It may seem to shut out
people of other tongues and nationalities, but language
and nationality are not the final marks of a people. Israel
was to speak other tongues and be called by other national
names, but this was not to destroy the essential unity of
Israel.   What called the various peoples to the United
States?   Not the fact that they spoke the same language—
they did not. Not the fact that they came from the same
sorts of political conditions—they did not.   But they came
here because their hearts' language was the same. They
are now part of that great human influence which we describe as "the English speaking peoples."   And these are

not all; the English speaking people do not merely comprise those whose native tongue is English, but those in generations yet to come whose adopted tongue shall be English—for there are some elements in God's good purposes for the human race that require the English tongue for their promulgation.

Even the Chosen People Stand Condemned For Their Disregard of God's Just Law

These are conditions that have come about without our collusion or support, indeed they have come about in spite of our utmost opposition. So that, even if we would, we cannot sing a paean of praise to the British people or to the American people. God has done great things **through** them and **for** them, but that they themselves are or have been great is a claim we cannot make. We cannot build a boast for ourselves out of work which God has performed according to His promise. When I think of the oppression of the people of Britain in former times and now, of the darkness that so long lay upon that people, of a feudal aristocracy fighting and feasting while the families of England languished in poverty; when I think of little English children driven to the first factories before daylight and kept until after dark, condemned all their life long to ignorance, all to build the great British commercial fortunes; when I think of social and ecclesiastical dignities and rulerships built upon the brewing of beer and the distilling of whiskey; when I think of their promised rule of many lands fulfilled by the Providence of God, only to be turned to selfish extraction of wealth; when I think of the terrible struggle Britain's best men made for the least of human reforms, only to be killed, ostracised, broken-hearted for their efforts—when I think of the blood which Christian England has spilt of her choicest saints, I cannot sing a paean of praise to Britain. No. This truth of Israel is not pro-British.   The Bible's lash on Israel's sins is a grievous thing, and forbids all boasting.

And when I turn to America and remember the venial character of much of our public life, of our intense engrossment with material pursuits; when I think of the vast economic slavery that still remains, of our rapid division into antagonistic social classes, of our lawlessness, our violence, our corruption in high places and low, our shameless surrender to sex, our descent to dirt in drama and literature, our hysterical moronic delight in the return of whiskey, our trampling of the Lord's Sabbath, our national supercilious sneer at religion, our pagan philosophy of dishonest success, our dollar aristocracy, our teeming millions of pauperized citizens—**please don't tell me that the truth which enables me to see these things is a truth invented to glorify them!** The truth of Israel is not and never can be the exaltation of man!

And yet—these are God's people! You read in the Old Testament their endless record of wrong-doing—you are amazed that they continue to be God's people.   And it is so you see them at the present day—as they were of old—having the highest privileges, making the lowest use of them.   Yet God goes on doing great things through them, and we as Bible students know that the purpose of God will yet be fulfilled in them, and that the growing pressure of divine judgments upon us indicates that the time of fulfillment is drawing near.   For the final word concerning us is not 'if you will;" it is **"you shall."** We have not been drawn from the ends of the earth to the ends of the earth only to defeat the will of God for the world through us.   No! He **will** do His will, and we **shall** do it. So, let no one harbor the thought that the aspect of truth which we espouse has for its purpose the glorifying of men or nations, or race—it glorifies God's purposes as they are to be fulfilled through men. The highest justification of man's existence—and we are constantly cheating ourselves of it—is that we shall be vehicles of God's earthly purpose.

In the Isles Our People Found Their God and Exalted Him In Their Thought

To return to our main theme. We think we know the routes and the times and the manner in which our fathers came from Palestine to the Isles. We know the racial elements which composed the peoples from whom America drew her sons. I should not omit to say that along with Israel, over all these routes, came other people also. These great migrations were not confined to the Israel people. On the flanks and in the wake of Israel there always were others. When Israel came out of Egypt there was a mixed multitude with them, always ready to complain, always ready to return to the leeks and onions of Egypt, never able to see God's hand in events, and the first to hold rump conventions and elect opposition leaders. When Israel came out of Assyria during the troubles of that empire, it is not unnatural that many Assyrians followed too. The road was open. Peace and safety lay farther on. No wonder many people left, and kept resourceful Israel company on the way, at length settling themselves across Europe in places that pleased them. Israel is not the only Eastern race we can identify in Europe today. The friends of Israel in those ancient lands and times are friends still, and ancient enemies of Israel continue their enmity in their modern homes. The picture today is about the same as it was in olden times, save that now Israel is no longer at the mercy of any enemy—God's promise of power and independence and progress to Israel has been fulfilled. And larger fulfillment waits on Israel's return to God. That is a point we always return to—God has fulfilled His word to us, we have not fulfilled our word to Him.

As to Israel's life in Britain we need not speak lengthily now. It is open to all who care to read. In spite of grievous faults, religion was always a living concern in Ireland, Scotland and England. The Bible as a people's Book first took its rise in England. The throne and commerce are founded on faith in God. As you stand in Westminster Abbey at the place where the Kings and Queens are crowned, you read in letters arching the chancel this great agreement and confession—"The kingdoms of this world are become the Kingdom of our Lord and of His Christ," an absolute declaration of the Kingdom of God on earth superseding all other kingdoms. The rude stone that lies beneath and within the ancient Coronation Chair is held by fond tradition to be the stone brought by Jeremiah, to Ireland, the veritable "stone pillar" whereat the Kings of Israel were crowned. And sure it is that the shout "God Save the King" that arises at the coronation is a literal cry of ancient Israel. And the known history of that ancient Stone of Scone renders it one of the Empire's choicest possessions. There is another stone in Israel, the center of a nation's reverent regard—we call it Plymouth Rock. But I said Commerce, too. One reads above the Royal Exchange in London, "The earth is the Lord's and the fulness thereof." Thus is the deep dignity of religious truth intertwined with the familiar things of common life. This is God's mark on Israel in

Britain. We cannot forget, we cannot evade, whatever else has come between, that thence we have our religion, our language, our democracy, our distinctive national ideals. We cannot deny our history.

How American Israel Was Nurtured and Prepared In the Midst of British Israel

But it is not the Israel in Britain that we seek today; we seek the Israel that was in Britain as a station **on its way to America.** American Israel can be traced in British Israel long before the Pilgrims crossed the sea. The first slender tendrils stretching over the wall were the explorers and adventurers in their restless search of the western ocean. They were led by a way they knew not to find a land they had never known. God was making paths in the sea against the time when Israel should be ready to come. And He was already nurturing in the central shires of England a life that should move them to come. As many times before in Israel's life, priestly and kingly power in England became oppressive. The Lollards arose, then came the Brownists, Separatists and Puritans, and with them a host that was friendly to liberty of conscience. The University of Cambridge was a center that fed the intellect of this newforming branch of Israel which all unaware of its destiny was growing in the midst of Israel in the Isles. A state of mind was forming which not only led to the flight of the Pilgrims but to Cromwell's Revolution which interrupted the kingly succession for twelve years. These divisions were implicit in the steady formation of the root of American Israel in the very midst of British Israel.

Preparatory Providences at one side of the main stream of events were not lacking. Spaniards opened up

the coast lands of the South and founded in Mexico a
flourishing civilization with universities and cathedrals
and great wealth of gold long before the Pilgrims came—
but the land was not for them. Frenchmen, fired by religious zeal for Indian souls, pushed through to the Upper
Lakes and far down the Father of Waters—but the land
was not for them. Dutchmen founded New Amsterdam,
a goodly people and a blessing to these shores—but the
land was not for them. The cavaliers of England came
to Virginia, with the state religion and high degree of
birth, British power behind them and Anglo-Saxon ideals
within them—but not yet was the land ready for them.
These all were instruments of a Preparatory Providence,
opening the way for the smallest and weakest and least
ambitious of all the invasions which because it was the
strongest spiritually, was to define the character of America. There were other Providences, unknown at the time
but immensely important later.

How minutely God works when His own purposes
are on foot! There was a perfidious Englishman who be-
trayed the confidence of some Indians of Massachusetts,
and seized them, carrying them off to sell as slaves in
Spain. But one of them, named Squanto, escaped, made
his way to England, learned the language, and was afterward by the kindness of an English merchant returned
to his native shore. Keep in mind for a moment this instrument of the Divine Providence, Squanto the Indian.

There were other Providences at work. As this
growing branch of Israel in the English shires grew more
and more interested in spiritual religion, a religion that
should be free of the stultifying appendages of a worldly
ecclesiasticism, they more and more incurred the displeas-
ure of the authorities in Church and State. And they had

never been able to undergo the period of incubation necessary to develop them into a loyal fellowship, had they
not been given special protection from harassment and
arrest. Now, it happened that where these like-minded
seeds of American Israel lived, at Scrooby manor, which
belonged to the See of York, one William Brewster was
bailiff and postmaster, a man who was not willing to hunt
down his neighbors who were called Puritan because they
sought a purer worship of God. And so the seed grew
unmolested. This man was succeeded by his son, William Brewster, who thirty years later became the famous
Elder Brewster, of Plymouth Colony, New England. In
his turn, he too used his office, his wealth and his social
position to protect his worshipping neighbors from trouble.
As a young man he had been secretary to William Davison who was Secretary of State to Queen Elizabeth, and
had accompanied Davison to Holland where he observed
the brave Hollanders in arms for the freedom of religion,
which they won. Doubtless here was the seed of the later
flight of the Puritans to Holland. On his return to Scrooby,
Brewster would tell of Holland. The little Puritan church
met in his barn. Thither came Rev. John Robinson, a
name immortal in the spiritual annals of America, and
William Bradford, afterwards Governor of Plymouth
Colony. Thus the quiet incubation of the leaders of Israel
to the farther West went on, and when the force of persecution could no longer be evaded, they were not like
frightened, scattered sheep, but a strong federation of
Christian families gathered in a church that was also
an economic unit, with a pastor like John Robinson and
leaders like Brewster and Bradford. For we must never
forget that the real beginning of America was a little
believing church. And we should remember the Providence that, in spite of kings and prelates, allowed that

little church to be gathered. And so they sought freedom in Holland. They were not rude, unlettered peasants. They were many of them graduates of the ancient English universities and able to read their Bibles in the original Greek and Hebrew. But, being gentlemen, scholars, men of peace, they lacked one element necessary for the rude work of the pioneer on a barbarous shore.

The Classic Providence Attending Their Flight To The New World

So, behold another wonder of the Divine Providence. There was a man of Lancashire—the same country from which George Washington's forebears came—by name, Miles Standish. Disinherited because of his Puritan sympathies, left without property though sprung of a wealthy family, Miles Standish had gone to Holland to offer his sword against the Spaniard in the fight for a free Christian faith. He rose to the rank of Captain. When finally the truce came, Captain Miles Standish wandered to Leyden, the very city where the little Puritan church of Scrooby had settled a year before. Whether he joined the little church, we do not know; my opinion is, he did not; he was a soldier, not a theologian. That little church had enough theologians. God was giving them a soldier who could arrange their self-defense in the new wilderness, a Joshua for their Moses. And when that little church had found to its sorrow after ten years of life in Holland, that the work of getting a living among a strange people can take too much out of the life of the soul; when they found that religious liberty in a free country can exist side by side with an appalling amount of religious indifference; when they found the Dutch disregard for the Sabbath too heavy for their consciences to bear; and when they had become

thoroughly alarmed by the effect of Continental life, even
at that early day, upon the minds and morals of Puritan
boys and girls—for these reasons, written down by themselves, they decided to go away to the wilderness of
America.   There they would rear an exterior community
life more representative of their interior spiritual life—
and Captain Miles Standish went with them.   Every
American school boy knows this gallant captain's exploits
in behalf of the little beleagured garrison of God at Plymouth Rock.

These are Providences as marked as any that attend-
ed Israel in the migration from Egypt.   And there were
more.   When they sailed west they carried a patent for
lands in Virginia.   They would not have been happy in
Virginia—they would have found many of the same conditions that irked them in England and Holland.   And
so, winter and storm drove them on Cape Cod; their master mariner would take them neither to the Dutch at New
York nor to the English at Virginia; they were compelled
to settle on the bleak shore of the north.   They came ill-
equipped for strife, and so they found this land they had
not sought had been denuded of Indians by a plague several years before, so that the immediate territory was
uninhabited.   And then, not long after, ignorant of almost
all the ways to preserve their lives in that new country,
losing nearly half their scanty number by death in a few
tragic weeks, who should come into their settlement one
day but the Indian Squanto!—it was his old home—he had
found all his people slain by the plague—and remembering
the kindness he had received at English hands across the
sea, hands that had rescued him from slavery and returned
him to his native coast—he paid the debt of kindness, and
taught the Pilgrims how to plant the corn, how to fertilize

the rows with dead fish, how to do a score of necessary
things, and became their potent ambassador of peace to
the powerful Indian chiefs round about.   Truly, "God
works in a mysterious way, His wonders to perform."
Our history is in reality a continued Bible with God's
miracles never absent.

Who were these Pilgrim Fathers They called themselves "the seed of Abraham, God's servant, and the
children of Jacob, His chosen."   It is so written in their
own records. They called themselves "a vine out of Egypt
into this wilderness." These are their words. They used
the old Israel word "led," not "driven"—denying that
either England or Holland had "driven" them out. Their
passage hither was speeded by the great Israel texts. They
braced themselves in trouble with the great Israel promises. They allotted their land as Israel did. They purged
their settlement of blood and crime after the counsel of
Moses, the lawgiver of Israel. The Israel blessing of long
life was vouchsafed them: of 51 deaths recorded of persons
who came to the Colony during the first ten years of its
settlement, only four were under 80 years of age,
the youngest being 73 years. Fifteen of them were over
90 years old, four of these over 95.

Moses, when Israel was brought out of Egypt was
tremendously impressed by the mighty character of the
event.

"Ask now," he challenged. "Ask from one side of
heaven unto the other, whether there hath been any such
thing as this great thing is, or hath been heard like it?

"Did God ever essay to go and take him a nation
from the midst of another nation, by tests, by signs, and
by wonders, and by war, and by a mighty hand, and by

a stretched out arm, as the Lord your God did for you
in Egypt?"

Parallels Between Israel and the United States
Are Both Striking and Continuous

Every man must write according to what he knows,
but we could tell Moses that the same mighty things occurred when this American nation was taken out of the
midst of another nation. The canon of the Bible is closed,
but the work of the God of the Bible goes on.

Being of Israel, these forefathers of ours proceeded
in all their plans after the pattern of Israel. Let us always
remember that the planting of America, in the strain that
determined our country's character was a spiritual planting. The fathers who planted this nation were Christians.
They came here as Christians. They came because they
were Christians. They came on a specifically Christian
venture. Get it fixed in your mind, beyond the power of
any false history to erase, that the planting which determined the genius of this nation was a Church—not a town,
not a colony, not a trading or exploring venture, not a gold
rush, but a Church. A little Pilgrim Church crossed the
sea for the sake of its church life—that is the true origin
of our United States.

See how closely **the parallels run between Israel and
the United States.** There is a striking similarity in **the
beginnings** of both. When Israel of old came out of Egypt
—from the continent of Africa to the Continent of Asia—
in a free parliament of their rulers, and in a free convention
of their people held at Mt. Sinai, by individual vote, they
elected Jehovah the Head of the State. It was a distinct
and solemn national act. And when American Israel came
out of the Continent of Europe to the Continent of Amer-

ica, they too made a Covenant with Jehovah, they drew up national documents of agreement with Almighty God. And, my friends, you and I as members of the nation are bound by what our nation has officially done. Let me show you the cords by which we are bound, and which will strongly hold us.

There is a little shallop tossing on the Atlantic near the tip of Cape Cod. And there encompassed by the waters, ere yet a single foot was pressed on Plymouth Rock, our fathers called a solemn convocation in the Mayflower's stuffy cabin and drew up the Mayflower Compact. . . . "In the Name of God. Amen. We whose names are underwritten, having undertaken for the glory of God and the advancement of the Christian faith, a voyage to plant the first colony . . . do by these Presents, solemnly and mutually in the presence of God combine ourselves into a civil body politic." **That was the beginning of our politics**—"In the Name of God. Amen."

The Testimony of Our National Documents To the Fact That America Is Covenanted To God

With increasing accessions from the godly people of the old lands, the number of the colonies grew to four, and federation became desirable. A man of God drew up the Articles of Federation. . . . "Whereas, we all came into these parts of America with one and the same end, namely, to advance the kingdom of our Lord Jesus Christ and to enjoy the liberties of the Gospel in purity we therefore conceive it our bounden duty . . . that as in nation and religion, so in other respects, we be and continue one." **That declaration made us a People.** It was the forerunner of all our government. What a descent we have made since then.

Now, in these lectures we have seen the great division which occurred between Judah and Israel over the matter of taxation, and how Israel rebelled against the throne of David and declared its independence, setting up a separate government. The same thing occurred with Israel in America. The British government forgot that the Colonists were British men, and adopted the strange unBritish policy of taxation without representation. Our fathers were 13 Colonies now, as there were 13 tribes in Israel. And again there came a mighty division in Israel —the Colonies revolted against the rule of England. And determining to do this, they produced another great Covenant Document, The Declaration of Independence, and there once more their allegiance to Almighty God is declared. We sometimes hear today an agitation toward "putting God in the Constitution," and it is implied that we are a Godless nation because Deity is not mentioned in the Constitution. But the Constitution is not our greatest national document. The Mayflower Compact made us a Civil Body Politic. The Articles of Federation made us a People. The Declaration of Independence made us a Nation. All of them are based on the people's allegiance to God. Not one of them ever has been or ever can be amended. The Constitution is a blue print of our administrative political machinery—it can be and has been amended from time to time; it is a changing instrument; it need not declare so unchangeable a condition as our rightful allegiance to God.

I often wonder how many Americans see the four great Characters, the four great Attributes of God, in our Declaration of Independence. Let me show them to you in four brief passages. (1) "The separate and equal station to which the laws of Nature and of Nature's God entitle them." There we acknowledge **the God of Nature, Cre-**

ator of **Heaven and Earth.** (2) "All men are endowed by
their Creator with certain inalienable rights." There we
acknowledge God the Father of mankind. (3) "We, therefore, the representatives of the United States, in General
Congress assembled, appealing to the Supreme Judge of
the world for the rectitude of our intentions." There we
acknowledge **God, the Moral Governor of the earth,** beneath whose awful hand we hold dominion over the land
and the people. (4) "And for the support of this Declaration, with a firm reliance on the protection of Divine
Providence, we mutually pledge to each other our lives,
our fortunes and our sacred honor." There we fervently
acknowledge **God, the Providential Guide, and Protector,
and Savior of Peoples.** There, my friends, in the Compact, the Articles, and the Declaration, is the three-fold
cord of solemn obligation which binds us to the Law of
God. Our Patriotism and our Religion grow on the same
stem. Out of our own mouths are we judged.

Just as in ancient Israel some of the people could
not follow the revolt against David's throne, so some
Americans could not follow the Colonies in the Revolution, they could not bring themselves to fight against the
old home. And these went to Canada and built up the
great Dominion to the North. And so, like Israel of old,
here are two governments, two nations, of the same people, living side by side. And today, thank God, the bond
between is peace and understanding. Once again in our
history a division was sought—there was a great Civil
War; but the divine divisions were now complete; a
Union that never fully existed before was forged indis-
solubly in the fires of that civil strife. **There are no more
divisions on God's agenda.**

The Testimony of Our Seal, Our Statesmen To the Israel Quality of the Nation's History

Are these national documents but ancient committ-ments of an earlier generation of whose religion we are slightly ashamed today, of whose convictions young men with glib tongues and plastered hair like to make fun? No, this Israel strain has persisted down the generations, even though the Nation at large seems to have forgotten its destiny because it has forgotten its God. We call this "God's Country"—but we do not always know the truth that lives in these words. And yet some have always known. George Washington knew. He called this "the second land of promise." At the close of the Revolution, when he laid down his conquering sword, he said, "My gratitude for the interposition of Providence . . . increases with every review of the momentous contest." And when they made him the First President, he said: "It would be peculiarly improper to omit, in this official act, my fervent supplications to that Almighty Being, who rules over the Universe. . . . No people can be bound to acknowledge and adore the invisible hand, which conducts the affairs of men, more than the people of the United States. Every step by which we have advanced to the character of an independent nation, seems to have been distinguished by some token of providential agency." Hear Abraham Lin-coln say that he was but "an humble instrument in the hands of the Almighty, and of this, His almost chosen people." Lincoln's mind stumbled at the fact—He did not know the Identity, but his heart told him aright. His mind was full of the Providences which made him think of this people as "God's **almost** chosen people"—but God makes no **"almost"** choices. And so, if we had hours we might spend them hearing the same testimony from the

lips of American prophets down to this day. As a people
we are no more worthy than any other people, it may be
that because of our neglect of them we are less worthy
than any people; but true it is nevertheless that great Covenants of profound influence on the earth have been fulfilled through us, the glory whereof belongs to a Cove-
nant-keeping God.

And so we say that the descent of this American
nation is from Israel of the Ten Tribes. Just as truly as
Israel came to the Isles, it came also to America. And in
much the same way. Israel came separately in groups
into the Isles as Danes, Saxons, Angles, Jutes. Israel came
in separate migrations to America as Britons, Germans,
Scandinavians and others—indeed, from every land Israel
came under other national names. And many beside Israel
came. Israel's enemies, and the enemies of law, and the
enemies of freedom, and the enemies of religion and justice, too. We have again in this land Israel's ancient
problem, how to establish Israel's law and Israel's peace
above the opposition of the mixed multitude. We have
reached a crisis in that respect. Up from the murky depths
of the underworld of the human soul have come every
noisome moral pestilence and every subversive force, in
the full strength of political power and money power and
satanic control of the Press, the Screen, the Stage and the
Platform. These now expose themselves freely and boast-
fully and claim that they at last have won the land. We
know it is not true. We know their present power is only
the measure of our own faithless forgetting of our origin
and our responsibility. And we know what the end
will be.

My friends, this is no modern form of fanaticism.
This is not religious peculiarity run wild. This is the most

fully provable public truth we know. The United States today represents one great body of Israel, bound by Israel's responsibility, fulfilling Israel's destiny. The marks of Israel are on us everywhere. Our Eagle is an Israel emblem—"As an eagle stirreth up her nest, fluttereth over her young, spreadeth abroad her wings, taketh them, beareth them on her wings; so the Lord alone did lead Israel, and there was no strange god with Israel."

When the moment came to choose the design for the Great Seal of the United States, Benjamin Franklin, Thomas Jefferson and John Adams, were chosen as the committee. I think it is one of the most remarkable passages in our history that both Franklin and Jefferson—**professedly freethinkers**—proposed designs having to do with Israel—Franklin proposing Israel safely crossing the Red Sea while the hosts of Pharaoh were engulfed, and Jefferson proposing Israel being led by the pillar of cloud by day and the pillar of fire by night. The Department of State issued a brochure on the history of our Great Seal, written by the Custodian of Documents in the Library of Congress, and the only book quoted in that work was the book of Professor Totten, who was one of the earliest advocates of our truth in this country.

And then look at the Seal which finally evolved. What do you find on it? On the obverse side you find the Eagle with thirteen stars above its head, 13 letters in the motto which flutters on a scroll from its beak, 13 paleways in the shield on its breast, in its right talon an olive branch with 13 leaves and 13 olive fruits, in its left talon 13 arrows fledged with 13 feathers. Here are seven sets of 13s on one side of our Great Seal. I will say it for the benefit of superstitious that 13 is the lucky number of the United States, and has been so all down its history.

And 13 was the number of the Tribes of Israel. And the 13th Tribe of Israel was Manasseh, whose name means "forgetfulness," and if there has ever been a people forgetful of all its past, it is this last, this 13th, this Manasseh-Israel people in the United States.

*Look at our Great Seal again. Whence do we get the Olive as our national flower? It is the sign of Israel everywhere throughout the Scriptures. Turn to the reverse side—you see "a pyramid unfinished." What is a Pyramid doing in the United States of America? We thought Pyramids belonged to Egypt. Well, here on the Great Seal of the United States is a Pyramid of 13 courses of masonry, and above it, floating in the Glory and having emblazoned on it the All-Seeing Eye, is the capstone of the Pyramid which never was set—"the chief cornerstone" spoken of by Our Lord as the stone which the builders rejected. That headstone of the corner, the apex stone, was never set on the Great Pyramid of Egypt, it has not yet been set on our national pyramid—but it hovers there on our Great Seal, it floats there in the Glory, as if awaiting the moment when it shall descend to complete our national structure with a divine completion. A Pyramid on the United States government Seal? It should occasion no surprise. It was Israel genius that built the Great Pyramid, and set therein its mathematical confirmation of divine truth for a scientific generation to read. The Pyramid and the Olive, the stone which the builders rejected and the All-Seeing Eye, the effulgent rays of the Divine Glory, and through it all the number thirteen— my friend, **a Bible-reading shepherd in the desert of Mesopotamia, who had never heard of the United States, would say on seeing our national emblems, "Surely this is**

---

*See page 201, "God's Covenant Race."—Anderson.

the people Israel!" And all this came about without knowledge, without intent, on the part of the statesmen who
designed it.   Truly, it is a most remarkable circumstance.
But Israel must be Israel wherever her sons abide.

The Covenant of Israel Is Being Fulfilled In the Manifest Destiny of the American People

I could entertain you for a long time with scores of
these marvelous coincidences, and in their aggregate I
think they work a sense of awe within your minds.   But
as I have said before in these lectures, our contention rests
on nothing merely human.   We do not build on such
flimsy foundations as a so-called "Nordic theory."   We
do not draw our strength from boastful racial egotism.
The Covenants of God set forth at length in Holy Scripture—**there is the rock** of this faith.   And though the track
of Israel from Assyria to the Isles were lost to us, and
though the Providence of God in our history were absent
from our national records, yes, even though no Israel
emblem had ever appeared on our arms, escutcheons and
seals, yet from the Covenants of God, and their present
operation on our people, I should know **who we are and
what we are here to do.**   For you must know, my friends,
that these Covenants are absolute; God has said that He
will never change or annul them.   He has said that they
shall stand as long as the sun and moon endure.   But they
have these optional clauses: if we live within the national
Covenant with God, it will be to our blessing; if we do
not live within the Covenant, it will be to our correction.
But the Covenant is always in force; nothing that we will
do can annul it, and God **will not annul it.**   His will is
always being done.   Make no mistake about that—God's
will is done.   We cannot defeat it.   His will is being done.
If not that part of His will which should have meant our
peace and prosperity, then that part of His will which

means our correction. If His will is not done **through us,** then it shall be done **to us.** And correction is as much a part of God's covenant with us as blessing is. He is still doing His part, as He said. The supreme proof I have that we are still God's Covenant People, though we have failed of our part, is that we are still within His correction. The clause of chastisement is operating. God's will, stopped on the right hand, is coming through on the left hand. If God cast off His people whom he foreknew, He would have broken His contract with them, He would have annulled His promise, and let us drift, and His covenant would not now be in force. But **it is in force, and what irresistible force! The earth verily trembles under it.** The Apostle wrote that "it is a fearful thing to fall into the hands of the living God." A Vice President of the United States said, "It is a fearful thing **to fall out of** the hands of the living God!" We are still in His hands. And this correction will continue until it accomplish the end whereunto it is sent. This nation must yet acknowledge the operation of God's hands, and set up God's justice throughout our system. And then, He that hath torn us will heal us, and He that hath wounded us will bind us up. And that day is coming as surely as this day has come, and the truth you have heard proclaimed here will help open the way for its coming. Oh, believe it, God will yet have the salute of our banners, and the allegiance of our people.

When the criers of our United States courts enter upon their duties tomorrow morning, they will stand up and all assembled there will stand with them, while the cry is made, "God Save The United States." That is our cry today, and it is not a hopeless cry—**God will save The United States.** For the kingdoms of this world **must** become the kingdoms of our God and His Christ, and He shall reign for ever and ever.

SECTION 2

JAMES H. ANDERSON was born in Salt Lake City, Utah. February 11, 1857. He became very active in civic and church work as a young man and continued so throughout his entire life time. When the Genealogical Society of Utah was organized in November 1894, he was its first secretary under Apostle Franklin D. Richards, president. In 1907 he was chosen a member of the General Board of the Young Men's Mutual Improvement Association, which position he held for over twenty years. By many he is considered one of the best students of history and scripture that the church has ever had. The volume of his writings from which these chapters are selected was published only a few months prior to his death. These articles are even more timely now than they were decades ago. "Truth is ageless."

FROM EGYPT 1486 B. C. TO AMERICA TODAY

The Fiery Pillar—Liberty and Loyalty—Racial Purity— Seven Times Punishment—Collapse of Law Danger —Dividing Israel—Maya Civilizations—Ten Tribed Nation—Racial Identity—The Birthright Heritage—Racial Destiny

"O trembling Faith, tho' dark the morn, a heavenly torch is thine!
While feebler races melt away, and paler orbs decline,
Still shall the fiery pillar's ray along thy pathway shine,
To light the chosen tribe which sought this western Palestine!"

Thus wrote Oliver Wendell Holmes in his poem "The Pilgrim's Vision." From Israel in "this western Palestine" in the present age, this favorite American poet harks back to the fiery pillar of Israel's deliverance from Egypt. The "pathway" still is lighted to him: the race still persists. Therein three vital factors are envisioned:

(1) Racial Purity.

(2) Racial Identity.

(3) Racial Destiny.

The scene depicted for thirty-four centuries ago is set forth in that best attested of all ancient historical records, the Bible, Exodus 13:20-22:

"And they took their journey from Succoth, and encamped in Etham, in the edge of the wilderness. And the Lord went before them by day in a pillar of cloud, to lead them by the way, and by night in a pillar of fire to give them light; to go by day and by night. He took not away the pillar of cloud by day, nor the pillar of fire by night, from before the people."

Assumed wise men of modern times may be incredulous as to the fiery pillar miracle by divine grace, but the culminating history of Israel as a divinely Cove-

(This and the following pages are selections from the writings of James H. Anderson. See "God's Covenant Race.")

nant Race from 1486 B. C. to today, sets forth a vastly greater scene of divine miracles. The mass of fugitive slaves fleeing before the well-organized army of the Egyptian Pharaoh were a frightened, servile body who had not yet come to recognize fitly the allwise omnipotent God whom their leader Moses subsequently announced at Mount Sinai.

Racial Growth

Prior to the Exodus, numbers of their race had escaped from bondage, and found freedom even in distant western Europe. Moses himself was an Egyptian fugitive for forty years "in the land of Midian"—the present Arabia—and returned as a divinely commissioned prophet to lead his people to freedom. And under that leadership those twelve tribes of slaves, in less than the ordinary life of a man, had become among their fellowmen an aggressive, dominating nation which even Egypt's Pharoahs feared and respected. In itself, that undisputed national transition stands a miracle of history—an event attained by divine guidance.

In their new home, there was born within them the spirit of liberty and loyalty and the genius of self-government. They were freemen under a beneficent divine leadership. It was Israel's God—the God of Abraham, of Isaac, and of Jacob—who gave the sublime motto inscribed on America's Liberty Bell: "Proclaim Liberty throughout the Land—to all the Inhabitants thereof" (Lev. 25:10). Antedating Athens and Rome, Israel's Palestine was the center of the world's highest civilization. Long prior to "the glory that was Greece and the grandeur that was Rome," Jerusalem was majestic in the civilized prosperity of her people. From the stupendous

Egyptian temple of Karnak for heathen worship, to the magnificent temple of Solomon at Jerusalem as a sanctuary for the true and living God, is a miracle of all time in the development of civilization through Jehovah's saving grace. The divine light of the fiery pillar was not extinguished.

Causes and Origins

But what of the poet's indicated modern event? In an age that is conspicuously distinguished from previous ages by its universal tendency to inquire into the causes and origins of all things, we may well inquire as to this. Note the race that in this age has become dominant in the world and holds pre-eminent leadership in the poet's "western Palestine" of America. It will not do to say that it "just happened" to gain its favored place only for the time being, in common rotation with other races. History will not justify such a conclusion; nor will the present mentality of Anglo-Saxon civilization permit such an assumption for the future. These declare the ultimate, continuing racial leadership of the Anglo-Saxon family. And why?

The designation Anglo-Saxon may not be as comprehensive to our thought as would seem desirable; for Celt and Dane, Saxon and Norman, are racially one. Deductions upon color of hair and eyes, skull measurements, or any other purely physical appearance, are beside the question. The mind, the mentality, may and do have a molding effect upon face and form. And the mind, the mentality, provide the test which the experience of man applies everywhere when race is mentioned. That test cannot be ignored as it relates to the Anglo-Saxon when this term is used in its broader sense.

Now, to causes and origins, beginning with the poet's inference. Who and whence the race?

Founding the Covenant Race

Centuries antedating the achievements of Moses there lived in the city of Ur of the Chaldees his ancestor, noted as one of the world's leading characters. The story opens in Genesis, in the first words of chapter 12:

"Now the Lord God said unto Abram."

Ur of the Chaldees was a stronghold of idolatry, as stated in scripture and confirmed by archeological discoveries to the present time. In the ancient record there is no suggestion that this idolatry was a step upward from its prehistoric status to a purer faith, as some modern philosophies would assert. To the contrary, it was a downward step from the primitive revelation of the invisible Creator. As the Apostle Paul explains in Romans 1:21-23:

"They glorified Him not as God, neither were thankful; but became vain in their imaginations, and their foolish heart was darkened. Professing themselves to be wise, they became fools, and changed the glory of the uncorruptible God into an image like unto corruptible man, and to birds, and to four-footed beasts, and creeping things."

Dominance of the prevailing worship as it was in Ur and throughout Chaldea would lead inevitably to a loss among men of knowledge of the true God. Some decisive action was necessary to secure for mortals a repository for the truth. Abram was a worshiper of the true God. To remain in his own city and among his own people meant that he would be overwhelmed. So the Lord said to him. Gen. 12:1, 2:

"Get thee out of thy country, and from thy kindred, and from

thy father's house, unto a land that I will show thee; and I will
make of thee a great nation, and I will bless thee, and make thy
name great; and thou shalt be a blessing."

Marvelous Destiny

A remarkable destiny for Abram's posterity is out-
lined in the 12th to the 49th chapters of Genesis, with a
culminating period of time "in the last days," as set forth
in the first verse of the 49th chapter. This destiny cites:
(1) A promised land; (2) a great nation; (3) a name
great; (4) to be blessed; (5) to bless those who bless, and
condemn those who curse; (6) to bless all the families
of the earth; (7) to have a numerous posterity; (8) Abram
to be the father of many nations; (9) his wife Sarah to
be the mother of nations; (10) to hold the sceptre of kingly power; (11) to do justice and judgment among mankind; (12) to be called in Isaac; (13) to possess the gate
of their enemies; (14) unrestricted dominion and blessing
to extend to all the earth; (15) to be held in an everlasting
covenant made by the Lord. A truly marvelous destiny
for the ages!

By way of a passing glimpse of the magnitude of the
promises foreshadowed, examine the first of these, the
land, as illustration. The boundaries are given in verse
18 of chapter 15:

"Unto thy seed have I given this land, from the river of Egypt
unto the great river, the river Euphrates."

Five times in the English translation of the Hebrew
Scriptures the words "river of Egypt" are from the Hebrew word **Nachal,** which means a winter torrent and
refers to the stream at El Arieh, south of Gaza. This
stream was the boundary line between Turkey and Egypt,
and is named in Bible maps as the "River of Egypt." But

in the description given to Abram in Genesis 15:18, the Hebrew word **Naharza** is used, meaning a river proper. It refers to the river Nile, in its long course through east central Africa. The area of land therein designated includes Egypt, the Sudan, Uganda, Abyssinia, the Somaliland and other parts, as well as Arabia, and reaches a northern boundary which takes in Palestine, Syria, and Mesopotamia. Not in the palmiest days of Solomon's kingdom was there a consummation of this land-promise in its entirety.

Miracle in Origin

An important feature of this covenant with Abraham is that it was unconditional to such of his lineal descendants as came within its scope, thereby constituting them a Covenant Race in world history and destiny. The covenant and unconditional clause are in Genesis, 17th chapter, verses 2, 4, 7, and 19, in the 22nd chapter verse 16, in the 26th chapter verses 3 and 5, and in the 49th chapter verses 22 to 26, which read:

To Abraham: "I will make my covenant between me and thee; . . . as for me, my covenant is with thee. . . . And I will establish my covenant between me and thee and thy seed after thee in their generations for an everlasting covenant, to be a God unto thee, and to thy seed after thee. . . . And God said, Sarah thy wife shall bear thee a son indeed; and thou shalt call his name Isaac; and I will establish my covenant with him for an everlasting covenant, and with his seed after him. . . . By myself I have sworn, saith the Lord, for because thou hast done this thing, and hast not withheld thy son, thine only son." Then to Isaac: "Sojourn in this land, and I will be with thee, and will bless thee; for unto thee, and unto thy seed, I will give all these countries, and I will perform the oath which I sware unto Abraham thy father. . . . Because that Abraham obeyed my voice, and kept my charge, my commandments, my statutes, and my laws." Further, to Joseph: "Joseph is a fruitful bough. . . His hands were made strong by the hands of the mighty God of Jacob . . . . who shall bless thee with the blessings of heaven: . . . the blessings of thy father (Jacob) have prevailed above the blessings of my progenitors unto the utmost bound of the everlasting hills; they shall be on the head of Joseph."

Motherhood had been promised to Abraham's wife Sarah. God had made that promise. He had changed Abram's name to Abraham, meaning "Father of a multitude." Abraham and his wife were advanced in years, beyond human prospect of parentage for them. He was an hundred years old, and she was ninety. They were human in their outlook, in measure at least. And they laughed. Read Genesis, 17th chapter 16th and 17th verses, and 18th chapter verses 9 to 15.

But right there Jehovah was revealed as the promise-fulfilling God. Isaac was born. The great race which was to be a blessing to all the families of the earth is rooted in a miracle!

To such as may wonder why Isaac was chosen instead of his elder brother Ishmael to bear the covenant, St. Paul explains in his epistle to the Galatians, chapter 4, verses 28, 30 and 31:

"Now we, brethren, as Isaac was, are the children of the promise. . . . For the son of the bondwoman shall not be heir with the son of the freewoman. So, then, brethren, we are not the children of the bondwoman, but of the free."

Liberty and Loyalty

"Take my yoke upon you," said Jesus to His disciples: "for my yoke is easy, and my burden is light" (Matt. 11:29, 30). In the divine plan there is a "yoke" —in other words an equipoise or just proportion of authority, responsibility, or obligation within certain lines, for a specified purpose. Jesus defines it as "yoke." To wear it worthily, a family purity of descent in the Abrahamic line was required. While the Covenant Race was to "bless all the families of the earth," yet a chosen line must carry an especial responsibility therein as a birthright. In the Covenant Race is that chosen line. So in Isaac must come, by divine decree, that heirship of the "son of the freewoman" named by St. Paul. The element of racial purity in the divine economy is thus revealed. To correlate in explanation: Freedom is an inalienable right. But love of liberty is not especially admirable if it takes the form of resentment of law. As restricted by loyalty to a given cause, it demands respect for law, if only for the sake of others; hence an application of the homely adage: "One cannot feed in a manger without wearing a halter."

Racial Purity

In this purity of family descent for the special obligation placed upon Isaac, the covenant heirship came to Abraham's second son, and likewise to Jacob, the second son of Isaac. Esau violated that rule of racial purity and thereby forfeited his heirship to bear the divine yoke for its special purpose. He contaminated his family descent by marrying wives of a forbidden line. Genesis 26:34, 35 reads:

> "Esau was forty years old when he took to wife Judith the daughter of Beeri the Hittite, and Bashemath the daughter of Elon the Hittite; which were a grief of mind to Isaac and to Rebekah."

Thus, by Esau's action, Jacob was the only one who, through preserving the purity of the family line which he did in his own marriage relation, could carry the Biblical birthright. Esau lost to himself that birthright by his disregard of the divine requirement, not by Jacob's craftiness. In this matter, the accusation of deceit against Jacob is gross injustice, based on omitting a consideration of the full Bible record. The favor of a just and all wise God is not earned by deceit or disobedience. Isaac's wife Rebekah knew this when she rightfully prevented her husband making a racial blunder. "Obey my voice" (Gen. 27:13), she commanded her dutiful son, and Jacob obeyed. God commended the righteousness of that mother and son by giving to Jacob the honored name of Israel —"ruling with God." So, also, in later years, Joseph observed the divine requirement by marrying a wife who was not of the forbidden Egyptian line, but who was of the Semitic family of Potipherah, priest or prince of On, or Heliopolis.

That is the Bible record. It establishes the first of the three vital features hereinbefore named, i. e., Racial purity. This racial purity became a fixed characteristic of the Covenant Race, for its divine mission. Racial purity is characteristic of the Anglo-Saxon race. In some Anglo-Saxon commonwealths, miscegenation is made the subject of criminal law.

Danger in Collapse of Law

Thoughtful and informed minds readily recognize as a fact that no calamity so threatens the foundations of a nation as the collapse of the law. This is true as it applies to the lawmaker, the administrator, or to the common evader. It is as applicable to national existence today as it was to national perpetuity thirty centuries ago. "Liberty," a popular and extensively distributed New York magazine, said recently, editorially, of the United States, "We are now the most lawless nation on the face of the earth." We also have it recorded in current history that in the Russian capital, Moscow, the name of Christmas Day was changed to a Slav word meaning "The Day of the Deposing of the Gods." On that day the Bolsheviki held high celebration. They marched through the streets with a stuffed figure marked "Almighty God" at the head of the procession, then burned the "Almighty God" in effigy. Whatever may be in store for the Russian nation under its present policy, world history has demonstrated this ineffaceable lesson: That the persons or nations who wish to live an undisciplined life had better start by getting rid of Almighty God. For, so long as He is here, there is Someone present who ought to be and who means to be obeyed.

Obedience to law is the unchangeable fiat of Nature. It is a glorious boon to humanity. The secret of all our material progress is in our recognition that the physical universe is a law-abiding system. All scientific advance depends on obedience to law. All high character depends on obedience to divine law. Indeed, obedience to God is the core of high character. The center of the great Nazarene's life was His obedience to the sovereign God. "Not my will, O Father, but Thine be done."

Kingdom of the Lord

As the great nation of united Israel approached a state of disobedience to the law of God, national disaster portended. In this particular instance the immediate forecast was for a divided nation. Solomon had been chosen "to sit upon the throne of the kingdom of the Lord over Israel," says the 5th verse of the 28th chapter of First Chronicles, in the Bible. The "kingdom of the Lord" is not a substitute for the Church of the Lord, nor is the gospel of the kingdom a substitute for the Gospel of salvation. These are two phases of God's great plan, and they run together in history. The gospel of the kingdom deals with national administration; the Gospel of salvation deals with Church membership progress. So in Israel there was the divine authority in religious matters in which the

Levites officiated, anciently, and the divine authority in temporal governmental matters assigned to the royal line of David.

Solomon's official prerogative was the sceptre or kingly line assigned to Judah (1 Chron. 5:2), and later put into effect by the choice of David as king. In David's progeny it was to remain until "the Lord God shall give unto Him (Jesus) the throne of His father David: and He shall reign over the house of Jacob forever; and of His kingdom there shall be no end" (Luke 1:32, 33). At the same assignment the Israel "birthright was given unto the sons of Joseph the son of Israel" (1 Chron. 5:2). One allotment was of the temporal sovereignty, the other of the "kingdom not of this world" but of heavenly ministration. So the Davidic line and the Levitical or Church administrations were measurably distinct, yet in harmony.

One Nation Becomes Two Nations

Moving toward the impending calamity, King David's royal son disobeyed the divine law. In the 11th chapter of the first book of Kings it is related that "The Lord was angry with Solomon, because his heart was turned from the Lord God of Israel; . . . he kept not that which the Lord commanded." And the Lord declared to him, "I will surely rend the kingdom from thee. . . . Notwithstanding in thy days I will not do it for thy father David's sake; but I will rend it out of the hand of thy son. . . . Howbeit, I will not rend away all the kingdom; but will give one tribe to thy son for David my servant's sake, and for Jerusalem's sake which I have chosen." The Davidic covenant provides that the royal kingly line of Judah shall remain throughout the centuries in David's family line.

The predicted rending of the united kingdom of Israel took place in the days of Rehoboam, son of Solomon, about 975 B. C. The house of Judah and the tribe of Benjamin, with whom the Levites in general remained, constituted the two-tribed kingdom in southern Palestine. The other ten tribes were the northern kingdom. Thus the rending of united Israel into a two-tribed nation and a ten-tribed nation, was the salvation of the Davidic line in Israel; for so angered were the Ten Tribes with excessive taxation as a burden in addition to other differences with Judah, that they would have exterminated the royal line of David and thus nullified the divine promise. But the Lord interposed by opening a different way. "What portion have we in David?" exclaimed the Ephramite leader of the Ten Tribes, now called the kingdom of Israel. "To your tents, O Israel!" was Jeroboam's battle-cry.

With the separation, the ten-tribed nation was led into idolatry by the setting up of two calves of gold as objects of worship (1 Kings, chapter 12). As to the two-tribed kingdom, in a letter to the Rev. Merton Smith on November 18, 1918, the Jewish Chief Rabbi says: "The people known at present as Jews are descendants of the Tribes of Judah and Benjamin, with a certain number of descendants of the Tribe of Levi. As far as is known, there is not any further admixture of other tribes." This does not preclude a small number from each of the other tribes having remained with Judah because of the idolatry of the Ephraim or Israel nation. The New Testament (Luke 2:36) says of Anna the prophetess that she was "of the tribe of Asher," one of the ten tribes comprising the nation Ephraim.

Because of their disobedience the name ISRAEL was taken from them (Hosea 1:9): "Ye are not my people and I will not be your God." Thus the identity of the Ten Tribes by the name Israel was lost. The locality of their chief abode apart from the scattering among all nations never was hidden; it always was in "the north" countries which, geographically speaking, are north and northwestern Europe, Asia and America, including the "isles afar off" of the Prophet Isaiah.

Yet it had been said that in the place, in "the north countries," where the name of Israel had been lost to the Ephraim or ten tribe nation, where the title of Isaac's Sons or Saxons had superseded it in the minds of all peoples, the name of God should be restored, and the children of Judah and the children of Israel should come together (Hosea 1:10, 11): "It shall come to pass that in the place where it was said unto them, Ye are not my people, there it shall be said unto them, Ye are the sons of the living God. Then shall the children of Judah and the children of Israel be gathered together."

Racial Identity

O Israel! "Still shall the fiery pillar along thy pathway shine." God's plan has worked out perfectly. Respecting the ten-tribed nation Ephraim, President Brigham Young, in a discourse in the Old Bowery, Salt Lake City, on May 31, 1853, said:

"The sons of Ephraim are wild and uncultivated, unruly, ungovernable. The spirit in them is turbulent and resolute; they are the Anglo-Saxon Race, and they are upon the face of the whole earth, bearing the spirit of rule and dictation, to go forth from conquering to conquer."

There may have been in the past three-quarters of a century some modification of the rough and ready pioneer

spirit prevailing when that address was made, but note
the identification.   At a later date, dealing with later
world developments, President Anthony W. Ivins, in a
General Conference sermon in the Tabernacle, Salt Lake
City, October 3, 1926, referred thus to the prevalent and
increasing Anglo-Saxon-Israel movement:*

"The thought is becoming almost universal in the British Isles
that Israel (the Ten Tribes) is there, where we have always known
them to be."

ANTHONY W. IVINS

The Anglo-Saxon race, using the term in its broader
sense, is vindicating every promise made to the lineal seed
of the house of Israel or ten-tribed nation as distinct from
the two-tribed nation.   By the tracing of history and of
Bible prophecy, Racial Identity of the Ten Tribes is established beyond successful controversy.   Quoting the words
of President Brigham Young: "They are the Anglo-
Saxon race."   No other race does or can lay claim to that

*See Addenda, page 245—"God's Covenant Race"—Anderson.

heirship. The Anglo-Saxon race alone has the proofs of heritage. The magnificent drama from Egypt to Jerusalem is being portrayed to the present hour in its intensified interest and grandeur. A further miracle of history is now in the record. To the disclosed factor of Racial Purity is added the proved factor of Racial Identity.

Spiritual and Temporal

We come now to a third scene. The Genesis story of creation presents two classes of control, the spiritual and the temporal. This is an unvarying rule of existence. In the divine plan for the Covenant Race, descendants of Abraham, Judah was entrusted with the sceptre of temporal power, leaving the spiritual leadership to the birthright line, which was placed with Joseph. It is recorded in 1 Chronicles fifth chapter that the "birthright was given unto the sons of Joseph the son of Israel;" and verse two reads:

"Judah prevailed above his brethren, and of him came the chief ruler; but the birthright was Joseph's."

Of Joseph's two sons Manasseh and Ephraim, the latter was set first in the blessing by the patriarch Jacob (Gen. 48:17-20); and the Prophet Jeremiah (31:9) gives the word of the Lord: "I am a father to Israel, and Ephraim is my first-born." The Lord further says of Ephraim (31:20, 31, 33):

"Since I spake against him I do earnestly remember him still; therefore my bowels are troubled for him; I surely will have mercy upon him. . . . I will make a new covenant with the house of Israel, and with the house of Judah. . . . This shall be the covenant that I will make with the house of Israel . . . and will be their God, and they shall be my people."

The sceptre line was placed in Judah through the

Davidic dynasty, but not fulfilled until centuries after the assignment in Genesis 49:10. Nor was it effective in the house of Judah during the "seven times" punishment of Leviticus 26th chapter, from the days of King Zedekiah 600 B. C. to 1914 to 1918, A. D. Then there loomed up the British royal line as the Davidic dynasty, without a competitor in that claim among the reigning dynasties of the earth.

*Taking the rule of the seven times chastisement as it affected the two-tribed house of Judah, and applying it to the ten-tribed house of Israel, or Ephraim nation, a remarkably informing and interesting situation is reached. This relates to the birthright heritage in its spiritual leadership. The seven times punishment of the house of Israel began approximately one hundred and twenty years before the similar condition with the house of Judah. Its termination therefore was one hundred and twenty years earlier than the end of the other in world history, or about 1800 A. D. Then what occurred?

Anglo-Saxon Supremacy

Take the dominating facts as these relate to the Anglo-Saxon race. The Napoleonic wars at the end of the eighteenth and commencement of the nineteenth centuries were racial rather than national in their effect. Napoleon I was of Italian descent, thus being racially Latin or Gentile as opposed to Anglo-Saxon or Israel. The recession of his efforts against the Anglo-Saxon was the achievement of Lord Nelson, British admiral, which gave to Great Britain the mastery of the sea, and established Anglo-Saxon supremacy in the world. That period and the closing of the seven times punishment for the

---

*See pages 8-9—"God's Covenant Race"—Anderson.

house of Israel synchronize precisely. So does the fact that the world expansion of the United States and Great Britain, the two great Anglo-Saxon or Israel nations, dates from that period. And so does the appearance of the modern prophet Joseph Smith, racially an Anglo-Saxon, as a claimant to the leadership of the birthright tribe, Ephraim. Like the dynastic claimant of the Davidic sceptre and the Anglo-Saxon claim to Israel's heirship, this claimant to the spiritual heritage of Joseph's birthright and the direct revealing of God's word in this dispensation has no competitor among mankind in this broad field. That undisputed certainty is a lesson of human salvation. As the Savior of the world, Jesus of Nazareth has no competitor in either promise or fulfillment. In the spiritual leadership, authority, and Gospel of Jesus Christ, is the one and only saving means of mankind. "The way for man is narrow, but it lieth in a straight course before him, and the keeper of the gate is the Holy One of Israel" (2 Nephi 9:41).

The Birthright Heritage

Measure the facts without prejudice. Joseph Smith was born in the State of Vermont in 1805. His parents were of Anglo-Saxon stock. Appealing to the Lord in 1820, he had a remarkable vision. He had recourse to the Bible as the word of God, and read the fifth and sixth verses of the Epistle of St. James, first chapter. Of this he says: "Never did any passage of scripture come with more power to the heart of man than this did at this time to mine." Of his vision he declares:

"I saw two Personages, whose brightness and glory defy all description, standing above me in the air. One of them spake unto me, calling me by name, and said, pointing to the other: *This is my Beloved Son. Hear Him.*"

Then, in 1823, there came to him an angel who informed him of a record of people who formerly dwelt on the American continent. In 1827 he was entrusted with that record. It informed him of his own lineal right to the birthright through Joseph of old (2 Nephi 3:14-16).

GROVE WHERE THE FATHER AND SON APPEARED TO JOSEPH SMITH

It was a revelation beyond any thought in his mind that the birthright line through Ephraim yet existed on earth. Thus the actual birthright heritage "according to the flesh" (Doc. and Cov. 86:8-11) was revealed to Joseph Smith as his. No man could trace it genealogically. Only God could reveal the fact. The record on gold plates which, with other articles, weighed about seventy pounds, was translated and called the Book of Mormon. It is a power-

ful testimony to the divinity of Christ and the miraculous
power of God. Compared with the Bible, in doctrine,
prophecy and history its harmony and accuracy are un-
impeachable. The developments of archeology in America and the condition of the aborigines on the American
continent bear witness to its historic truth.

God had promised a revelation of "the everlasting
gospel" (Rev. 14:6, 7) when "the hour of God's judgment is at hand," for "every nation, and kindred, and
tongue, and people." The prophet Joseph Smith received

ANGEL-HERALD
EMBODIMENT OF ANGEL BRINGING THE GOSPEL
REV. 14:6, 7.

that revelation for the time and purpose stated. In 1829 the divine authority held by John the Baptist and by the Apostles Peter, James and John was given him. The Church of Jesus Christ of Latter-day Saints was organized.

The divine prediction, frequently repeated, is that in latter days Israel shall be gathered as one people. In 1836, the heavenly messenger Moses gave to the prophet Joseph the keys of that gathering. The dispensation of the gospel to Abraham was one of spiritual growth in Israel's divine leadership. The prophet Joseph says the heavenly messenger Elias conferred upon him this power. God had declared there would be a "great and dreadful day" (Mal. 4:5, 6) which would call for His sending the prophet Elijah for the blessing of God's children of every age and time. That "great and dreadful day" is being recognized in present events. Joseph Smith tells how this heavenly messenger came to him with the divine word, for "all nations of the earth." That the force of this message is upon the world today, especially in genealogical research for blessing themselves, their ancestors, and their progeny, is beyond dispute, and in the very way indicated by the Lord. So it is with all the other visitations. There is no other claim in the world similar to that of the prophet Joseph Smith.

Revealing Power of God

Each and every claim made by him is of the revealing power of God, not of human wisdom or achievement. They are in accord with Bible record and promise. Men may disbelieve, but they cannot disprove a single claim. Today is the culmination of revealing the Racial Destiny of the Anglo-Saxon peoples. It includes every feature of the promises made to its founder Abraham.

You who are inquirers into the causes and origins of all things, why not inquire deeply into this record of development and claim? It will bring a sure testimony.

God spake to the patriarch Abraham, and Abraham obeyed.

God spake to the prophet Moses, and Moses obeyed.

God spake to many scripture prophets, and they obeyed.

God spake to the prophet Joseph Smith, and he obeyed.

Why not you, too? God has spoken in this dispensation. Will you hear Him?

The poet's "chosen tribe which sought this western Palestine," our America, has had its way lighted by the "heavenly torch" through the centuries. It is God's miracle through historic ages, going on until every knee shall bow and every tongue confess that Jesus is the Christ, to the glory of God the Father and the blessing of His children eternally; for

> "Truth shall conquer at the last,
>   As round and round we run;
> And ever the Right comes uppermost,
>   And ever is Justice done."

Some Study Questions

1. When and where was the covenant race founded?

2. What were some of the distinctive marks of destiny for this race? (Genesis 12th to 49th chapters)

3. Why is the Abrahamic covenant known as "an unconditional covenant"?

4. What action of Esau's caused him to forfeit his birthright?

5. Would marriage now by a Latter-day Saint into this same race (Hamitic) bring the same result to his posterity with regards to their right to the priesthood? Why?

6. What is the secret of all progress, material and spiritual? Why?

7. Discuss the fact that the Kingdom of the Lord is not a substitute for the Church of Jesus Christ, nor the gospel of the Kingdom a substitute for the Gospel of salvation.

8. Tell the story of the rending of the united kingdom of Israel.

9. When and how did some of the Israel people get established in America?

10. Discuss what happened to the northern kingdom or the ten tribe part of the twelve tribe Israel kingdom.

11. What historical evidence have we that God has literally kept His scriptural promises and prophecies to the Israel race?

12. What two classes of control are presented in the Genesis story of the creation?

13. Which of these does the British Royal Dynasty claim? Why?

14. Which of these does Joseph Smith and his people claim? Why?

QUERIES CONCERNING TEN-TRIBED ISRAEL

Myths regarding the Ten Tribes—Did not Return to Pal-
estine—The Apocrypha and History—Mission of
Elijah and World Crisis—Questions for Serious
Contemplation

"Ye shall know the truth, and the truth shall make you free"
(John 8:32).

Jesus was telling the Jews of the bondage which comes
from committing sin and remaining therein. Most of His
hearers on that occasion rejected His teachings. Yet He
had enunciated a vital principle. Those who persist in
error, mental or physical, are in the bondage of sin. The
measure of bondage is marked by the extent of the error.
To benefit by the lesson which Jesus was seeking to im-
press, it is necessary that wherever we are following erroneous notions we abandon the same, and accept the
truth. Full investigation to learn the truth is commendable; partial investigation merely to confirm preconceived
opinions leads to error.

At this particular period of existence, there is an immediate menace in erroneous notions. The world is face
to face with the greatest crisis of the ages. We are on
the verge of an hour of trouble, when the very destiny
of humanity is at stake. It bids us well to investigate
calmly and prayerfully our own position, and set ourselves
right where we may be at fault.

Plenty of misunderstanding exists in the world, sometimes within ourselves, sometimes with others. In a recently published book on religious leaders, this by an

author who claims twenty years diligent study, it is said of Joseph Smith and the Book of Mormon that in that book Joseph Smith "capitalized the old legend of the lost tribes" by placing these as the aborigines of America. Yet the Book of Mormon does not do so. It has the history of two migrations from the Old World to America. One is of a colony that came to this land many years before Jacob, or Israel, was born, having no reference to the ten tribes. The other migration is of a family belonging to one of the Israelitish tribes, which family came from Jerusalem one hundred and twenty years after the main body of the ten tribes had been carried away by the Assyrians. The Book of Mormon itself mentions the "lost tribes" as being elsewhere than in America, at the time of its record. Hence the story in the recent publication referred to is mythical, to say the least.

What About Fairy Tales?

It may be interesting to inquire whether there are prevalent among the Latter-day Saints erroneous myths, fables, and fairy tales as to who and where the ten lost tribes are. These tribes did not return to Palestine after the Assyrian captivity. The Jewish historian Josephus makes this clear and positive statement:

"The ten tribes did not return to Palestine; only two tribes served the Romans after Palestine became a Roman province."

Hence, the idea prevailing in the world for centuries that the Jews comprised all Israel, inclusive of the ten tribes, was in reality an error. There are many other ideas today that also must be classed as error, notwithstanding that they have become prevalent among us, in one way or another. (2 Nephi 28:14.)

When the writer of this essay was only fourteen years old, he was made a Sunday School teacher of a Bible class of boys about his own age. He had no "advanced" or modernistic views or any "private interpretations." He took the Bible for what it said as far as he understood it, sometimes referring to a Hebrew or Greek lexicon for a clearer meaning of the words in the King James translation. This has been his method ever since, in applying Bible statements; and it has kept him from some mistakes. As to the people of early days in Utah, his family were among those driven from Illinois as Mormons. He was born and reared among those early Nauvoo pioneers in Salt Lake City. He heard discussed probably all the fairy stories concerning the ten tribes accredited to Joseph Smith by those who wished some authoritative backing for their views. Among others of these fables was the Symmes hole or hollow earth theory; the fish-bladder or extended knob-on-the-earth suggestion; the chip-off-the-block or broken off piece of a star proposition; the North Pole or dumping of a vast body of people behind the icebergs story; and others equally as unsupported by history, prophecy, or native reason.

This boy also received at this time some good advice from a practical Latter-day Saint who had been a Church member from the days of Ohio. It was to this effect: That the religious theorists who backed one or the other of the explanations named often were charging to the Prophet Joseph Smith statements they personally thought he might have made, and later would insist that he did make them, when in fact he never thought of them. This was found by experience and inquiry to be true. Thus the fairy stories, myths, and baseless fabrications about the ten tribes grew and received credence with many who did not make reasonably thorough investigation of the Bible prophecies and statements regarding those people, nor of the plain developments of history. It is not easy to correct these errors, because of the very thought exemplified by the Jews when Jesus was speaking to them, and thus tersely and bluntly expressed by a prominent American writer of today, who says: "People like to be ignorant. Not only do people generally prefer to remain in ignorance of what is about to transpire in their lives, but often they have a subconscious animus against the person who attempts to make them wise."

It would be well to remember this human weakness when noting that results of an investigation of Scripture statements concerning the ten tribes of Israel can be summarized into the simple fact that they went into the "land of the north," and occupied it; that the name of God in the word Israel was taken from them or "lost," while at the same time they were fulfilling their prophetic destiny of blessing all the families of the earth; and that in the very place—that is, in the north country—where they lost the name, as noted by the Prophet Hosea and others, in the latter time that name would be restored to them, and then should "the children of Judah and the children of Israel be gathered together, and appoint themselves one head, and they shall come up out of the land."

The Apocrypha and Josephus

The history of the kingdom of Israel, or the northern kingdom, ends in the Bible in these words (2 Kings 17:18):

"Therefore the Lord was very angry with Israel, and removed them out of his sight: there was none left but the tribe of Judah

The words "tribe of Judah only," should read "house of Judah only," as the kingdom of Judah included the tribes of Judah and Benjamin, with many of the Levites. This kingdom continued to exist for at least one hundred and thirty-three years after the removal of Israel. In the Bible nothing more of Israel's history is told as history. Prophecy, on the other hand, has much to say of their future in their fulfilment of the promises and predictions made to Abraham.

The Apocrypha, however, carries this history of the ten tribes a little farther, and tells of what happened to them and of their great movement to the north—north of Assyria. The Book of Esdras (Ezra) tells us (2 Esdras 13:39-45) that these captives of Israel migrated to Ar-Sareth, a region in the south of Russia, northwest of Assyria and beyond. This migration began in a small way about a century after their main deportation. It had commenced before the destruction and carrying away of the kingdom of Judah by Nebuchadnezzar. A part of Israel had started on their migration out of the land of their captivity and into Europe before Judah ceased to exist as a kingdom. When the Jews returned to Palestine from that captivity, the main body of the Israelites were in Ar-Sareth, over a thousand miles from Babylon. This migration into Europe began by degrees at the time when the great Assyrian empire was falling before the rising of the new world empires of Babylon and Medo-Persia. Israel then seized the favorable opportunity of commencing an escape into Europe, and continuing it over a period of two centuries, until Asia was wholly abandoned by the main body. Here is the passage from Esdras, the last two sentences being a prophecy, seen in vision:

"And whereas thou sawest that He gathered another peaceable multitude unto Him;

"These are the Ten Tribes which were carried away prisoners out of their own land in the time of Osea the king, whom Salmanesar the king of Assyria, led away captive, and he carried them over the waters, and so came they into another land.

"But they took this counsel among themselves that they would leave the multitude of the heathen, and go forth into a further country, where never mankind dwelt.

"That they might there keep their statutes, which they never kept in their own land.

"And they entered into Euphrates by the narrow passages of the river. For the Most High there showed signs for them and held still the flood, till they were passed over. For through that country was a great way to go, namely of a year and a half, and the same region is called Ar-Sareth (the countries).

"Then dwelt they there unto the latter time.

"And now when they shall begin to come, the Highest shall stay the springs of the stream again that they may pass through; therefore sawest thou the multitude with peace."

There is yet another source of information which throws light on the subject. This is the writings of Josephus, who lived at the time of the final destruction of Jerusalem by the Romans in A. D. 70. It was in that year that the Roman general Titus turned over to Josephus the sacred records of the Jews, which had been kept in the repository near the temple. This historian says:

"So Ezra read the Epistle of Xerxes at Babylon to those Jews that were there. . . . Many of them took their effects with them and came to Jerusalem, but then the entire body of the people of Israel remained in that country, wherefore there are but Two Tribes in Asia and Europe subject to the Romans, while the Ten Tribes are beyond the Euphrates till now, and are an immense multitude."

Promises Planted in Children's Hearts

One further item, both of interest and value, is to be considered. In the Pearl of Great Price, where Joseph Smith's experience with the angel Moroni are related. Joseph states that the angel messenger said of the coming of Elijah the Prophet: "He shall plant in the hearts of the children the promises made to the fathers, and the hearts of the children shall turn to their fathers. If it were not so, the whole earth would be utterly wasted at His coming."

Who are the fathers? The ancient patriarchs to whom those promises were made, of course.

What promises are "planted in the hearts of the children?" The Lord's promises made to those patriarchs, "their fathers," for future years.

Whose hearts are now turning to the fathers in consequence of the "planting" of those promises? The children, or descendants of those patriarchs, including the ten tribes of Israel.

The conclusion is unavoidable, since that turning is by the Anglo-Saxon Celtic race, and no other. That race is making successful genealogical research beyond computation, thus aiding in opening the way for gospel ordinances for the dead. What are earnest Scripture investigators going to do about it? They have their choice. It is fairy stories, fables, mystical speculations, against prophetic and historic facts.

Again, as to the closing sentence of the angel's words as cited by the Prophet Joseph Smith: "If it were not so, the whole earth would be utterly wasted at His coming." Repeating here the words used in our opening statement: "The world is face to face with the greatest crisis of the ages. We are on the verge of an hour of trouble when the very destiny of humanity is at stake." Has the Lord permitted that crisis to come upon His children without doing His part relative to sending Elijah the prophet? Let us think for ourselves, remembering at the same time this one inescapable fact—"The word of the Lord fails not," either past, present or future.

It may now be well to do a little further serious thinking, for which the subjoined questions are presented. Permission has not been asked to use the name of our Brigham City brother who submitted the questions in a personal

letter calling forth the response that is here given; but
that is unimportant, since only the reply is used here.

Some Ten Tribes Questions For Thoughtful People

Dear Brother: Salt Lake City, January 29, 1927.
        Your note of January 27, 1927, received. The subject
to which you refer is a big one, and to put in written form
what information is available, would take some time. So,
to give an early response to your request, I shall make
merely a few suggestions, by some questions, until such
time as a personal conversation and investigation of the
standard doctrinal works of the Church afford a basis for
conclusions. In the meantime, some of my questions may
be abrupt because written hurriedly, but I have no such
intent. My desire is that the items called attention to be
discussed dispassionately, not with a spirit of disputation
and argument, for this spirit never results in learning the
truth in a satisfactory way.

        You ask me **my** opinion. I am not giving any. My
opinion, or that of any other man, purely as an **opinion**
is no better than that of Bill Brown or Tom Jones. The
facts are what we need.

        1. Why are some Latter-day Saints always after
the mysterious or fantastical?

        2. Why did the Jews look for a Savior who would
at that time wipe out the Roman power and give them
control when they were unfit to use it because of their
dogmatism?

        3. Why, in 1833, did some Mormons in Jackson
County look for the Ten Tribes to come at that time and
deliver them by overthrowing the Missouri mobocrats?

        4. Why, when the Saints came here to Utah, did
many of them refuse to build substantial homes because

they thought they were going right back to Zion in Missouri?

5. Why do some people say (as you quote), the Ten Tribes will come and "bring their own records with them?" I have heard that preached many times, but have never found a man who could produce that statement authoritatively, or anything like it. Where is it recorded?

6. Did the Jews bring with them the record of the Savior's life and visits as recorded in the New Testament? Or did other people than the Jews gather and preserve that record, while the Jews as a people decried it?

7. Did the Nephites, Lamanites, or American Indians bring the record of the Savior's visit on this continent? Or did somebody else get it when it had been hidden up? Would not these same Lamanites, or the early adventurers after the discovery of America, have destroyed it, if they had got hold of it?

8. Then, what basis of comparison have we for saying that the Ten Tribes, or any part of them today, have knowledge and possession of the record of the Savior's visit to them?

9. I have read somewhere that the Lord said that "teaching for doctrines the commandments of men" was "an abomination" in His sight. Is it any less an "abomination" when this teaching is by mystery-loving Mormons than by mystery-loving sectarian preachers who are deceiving the people thereby?

10. Some L. D. S. people assert that the Ten Tribes have with them some other Church than the one of which we are members, and have "their prophets" with them in that organization. Then what are they going to do with the Lord's statement in Doc. and Cov. Sec. 1, verse 30, respecting the Mormon Church, that it is now "the

only true and living Church upon the face of the whole earth?"

11. If the Ten Tribes, other than us, have "their prophets" with them, why do they have to come to Ephraim—that is, to the Mormon Church, to get their blessings?

12. Who is the prophet to Israel scattered to "the four parts of the earth?" Does not the Doctrine and Covenants, 110:11, say it is Joseph Smith, to whom was given the keys for that calling?

13. Are not the other prophets the thousands of such officers, missionaries and others, who have received their priesthood keys through Joseph Smith?

14. Who is the prophet to lead "the Ten Tribes from the land of the north?" Does not the Doctrine and Covenants, 110:11, say it is Joseph Smith, to whom was given the keys of that leading?

15. Are not our Latter-day Saint Elders of Israel, members mostly of the tribe of Ephraim, who was one of the Ten Tribes and of the leading tribe thereof in all the ages? These Elders have received their keys and calling from Joseph Smith, who had those keys. Are they not the prophets to the Ten Tribes for the "leading" of whom they have the keys?

16. When the Lord told Joseph Smith (Sec. 133:26) that "they who are in the north countries shall come in remembrance," did not Joseph Smith know that the "north countries" are northern America, northern Europe, and northern Asia?

17. Are not the Elders of Israel, with the divine prophetic calling which they bear, leading the tribe of Ephraim, the chief tribe of the ten, from these same north countries? Is not this an actual opening of "the leading

of the ten tribes from the land of the north" in fulfilment
of the mission divinely assigned to the prophet Joseph
Smith? The leading of the chief tribe of the ten, from the
days of the Prophet Joseph until now, is an indisputable
fact. Is not that fact a definite assurance of the following
in due time of the remaining nine tribes, to receive their
blessings "by the hands of the servants of the Lord, even
the children of Ephraim," the leading tribe of the ten
upon whom is "the richer blessing?"

18. Is not Ephraim being gathered, "two of a family
and one of a city" from among his fellow tribes in these
same north countries?

19. Is not Ephraim as we gather him, altogether of
the Anglo-Saxon Celtic race? And are we not impelled
to look for Ephraim's fellow tribes in the same race as
that from which he comes?

20. Does not the Anglo-Saxon race, even those of
that race in northern Russia, such as Finland, Latvia,
Esthonia and north Siberia, own all of the "north country" on earth?

21. You probably know that in Israel came the blessing of Abraham that in him and his seed should "all the
nations of the earth be blessed." Was the promise ever
made to any other than this part of the Abrahamic race?
Was it made to Ishmael, Esau, or Midian?

22. Were the Twelve Tribes divided into "two nations" (1 Kings 11:29-35; 12:16-20, 24), one known in
the Bible as Judah and Jews, the other as Israel, Joseph,
Ephraim, and the "seed of Isaac?"

23. Has not the Lord persistently recognized this as
the only division of the chosen race—two nations?

24. Does He not say (Ezek. 37:22), that in the latter
days they still are "two" nations in His sight, and that

in the latter days they shall become "one nation," and
"they shall be no more **two** nations, neither shall they be
divided into **two** kingdoms any more at all?"

25. Is not the tribe of Manasseh, to which Lehi belonged, one of the tribes assigned to the ten-tribed nation
of Israel, or Joseph, or Ephraim, or seed of Isaac, as it is
variously termed in the Bible?

26. Have you read the quotations by St. Paul, of this
nation of Israel, "In Isaac shall thy seed be called?" Have
you noted that the sons of Judah, or Judah's sons, in name,
has evolved to the common name Jews; while the sons of
Isaac, or Isaac's sons, has evolved into Saac-sons, or Saxons in conformity with the predictions in Genesis and in
the New Testament?

27. Have you noted that the "sons of Ephraim" in
the Bible is applied both to the tribe of Ephraim, and to
the nation of Israel, or Joseph, or Ephraim, and that on
page 670 of the Discourses of Brigham Young, used by
the Priesthood quorums, he says of the sons of Ephraim,
"They are the Anglo-Saxon race?"

28. Have you noted that when the Ten Tribes—
those who have not been called out as of Ephraim—
shall come to the birthright tribe of Ephraim for their
blessings, "they shall bring their rich treasures," not their
records? (Doc. and Cov. 133:30).

29. What race has got the rich treasures? What
race owns and controls, say four-fifths of all the coal, the
oil, the gold, the industrial wealth, the arable land, etc.,
of the earth? Is it not those who have the "rich treasures"
who will bring them?

30. Who said that when "the mountains of ice flow
down at their presence," the Ten Tribes must be viewing

those mountains from the North Pole, and not from the land south, from which they may look northward?

31. Who said that when the sea is "driven **back** into the north countries," the lands of the north shall not be brought to the south, and "the land of Jerusalem and the land of Zion be turned **back** into their own place" to the condition existing before the earth was divided, and the ice be melted by the natural warmth of the temperate zone? (Doc. and Cov. 133:24).

32. Who said the "mountains of ice" should be melted by the Ten Tribes, instead of by the Lord's power, when the mountains shall flow down at His presence?

33. Have the Jews preserved their identity, by mixing only to a limited degree with the other races. Hasn't the Anglo-Saxon race done the same? Doesn't the Englishman, the Scandinavian, the German, the Anglo-Saxon American, as a race, feel himself superior to the other races —"the head and not the tail" (Deut. 28:13)?

34. Isn't the Anglo-Saxon race a distinct people with their chief center of power in "the north countries," yet is at the same time scattered or "pushed together to the ends of the earth" (Deut. 33:17)?

35. I know the quoting of the hymn on page 386 of the L. D. S. Hymn Book, and the saying that Joseph Smith saw and approved it. The same hymn contains the statement how in the grave the "martyred Joseph lies," showing that it was written after the Prophet's death. But aside from that, is not President Brigham Young in the statement I have quoted from p. 670, as good an authority as a hymn, especially when it is known that no two people were closer than the Prophet Joseph and President Young in discussing doctrines?

36. The Doctrine and Covenants, Sec. 103:17, says

of us, "Ye are the children of Israel, and of the seed of Abraham" and "lawful heirs according to the flesh" (Doc. and Cov. 86:8-11). How many of those who discuss the subject believe that is true? Did we come from the Anglo-Saxon race, and did Joseph Smith himself?

37. The Doctrine and Covenants also says, "As your fathers were led at the first," etc. (Sec. 103:18). How were they led out of bondage; and was it by the authority of the Holy Priesthood?

38. Are the times of the Gentiles fulfilled? Jerusalem is no longer "trodden down" (Luke 21:24), hence is not this the Day of Israel, when people are divinely led to discuss the very subject of your letter?

39. Do we believe the Book of Mormon, which says "the more part of all the tribes which have been led away" are "upon the isles of the sea," especially referring to the western and northern coasts of Europe, but precisely what specific locality Nephi did not then know? (1 Nephi 22:4).

40. Do we believe that they who deliver Jerusalem in the latter days will come from the "north and the west" (there is no word for northwest in Hebrew, so north and west mean northwest) (Isa. 49:12), and realize that the British Isles are northwest from Palestine? Whence came the nation that delivered Jerusalem from the Gentile Osmanli dynasty (the body of the Turks being of Esau)?

41. Do we note that the opening of the Doctrine and Covenants (v. 1), separates the "islands of the sea" from the nations, as is done in several places in that book and in the Book of Mormon?

42. Do we realize that the Roman power never crossed the Rhine, or went more than a few miles north of the Black Sea, or into north Scotland, and hence that the

"north country" referred to in the Bible was the great "unknown north" covering more than half of Europe? Are we alive to history and to current events in the line of fulfilling prophecy, ancient and modern (Doc. and Cov. 88:79)?

43. Do we realize that the twelve tribes of Israel are to be gathered or unified into one national people (Ezek. 37:22) from which national unit they were sundered in 975 B. C. (1 Kings 11:30-32; 12:19, 20) and subsequent dispersion; and that the Apostle John was assigned the spiritual mission of that gathering or unifying of the twelve tribes the world over in the last days (Rev. 10:2, 8-11;

JOHN THE REVELATOR

Doc. and Cov. 77:14)? Are we alive to current events today, when, by some invisible spiritual force, the Judah nation and the Anglo-Saxon Celtic people of the north are becoming a racial unit in the eyes of the world, and the only race thus being recognized?

You will see now by these few questions what I mean when I say it is a big subject, not to be discussed with a word of dictum. I have not quoted the great volume of proofs of Bible prophecies fulfilled, nor have I expressed intentionally any opinion. I have given a list of questions hurriedly, and hope I have answered therein the two specific questions you asked, and also have furnished a basis for the good brethren to whom you refer considering the subject carefully. I have just one suggestion to offer: Notwithstanding any preconceived notions that may have come from what we may have heard somebody say as a guess or theory, let us leave "mysteries" to "Mystery Babylon, the mother of harlots," and get fixed in our minds the one fact of Bible, Book of Mormon and Doctrine and Covenants, that the Ten Tribes were lost only as to their identity and not as to their location, which has always been given as the "north countries" and the "Isles of the sea." The Lord has now begun to reveal their identity, first with the tribe of Ephraim, and then with the other tribes, when the time comes.

A hundred and fifty years ago the tribe of Ephraim could not obey the Gospel—the time had not come. The others of the Ten Tribes, though they may hear it preached by the Elders, do not receive the Gospel yet, because their time has not come. St. Paul says "blindness in part has happened to Israel," and he did not mean Jews. The epistle of the Apostle James is to "the twelve tribes which are scattered abroad," and "scattered abroad" does not

mean cooped up at the North Pole, "behind an impene-
trable wall of ice," as some of "the commandments of men"
taught for "doctrine" would have us believe.

In a letter to church missionaries by the Prophet
Joseph Smith, dated May 14, 1840, he said:

"If there is anything calculated to interest the mind of the Saints,
to awaken in them the finest sensibilities, and arouse them to enterprise
and exertion, surely it is the great and precious promises made by our
heavenly Father to the children of Abraham; and those engaged in
seeking the outcasts of Israel, and the dispersed of Judah, cannot fail to
enjoy the Spirit of the Lord and have the choicest blessings of heaven
rest upon them in copious effusions.

"Brethren, you are in the pathway to eternal fame, and immortal
glory; and inasmuch as you feel interested for the covenant people of
the Lord, the God of their fathers shall bless you. Do not be dis-
couraged on account of the greatness of the work; only be humble
and faithful. . . . He who scattered Israel has promised to gather them;
therefore, inasmuch as you are to be instrumental in this great work,
He will endow you with power, wisdom, might and intelligence, and
every qualification necessary while your minds will expand wider
and wider, until you can circumscribe the earth and the heavens,
reach forth into eternity, and contemplate the mighty acts of Jehovah
in all their variety and glory." "History of the Church" (official), Vol.
4, page 128.

With kindest personal regards, I am,
Yours truly,
J. H. A.

BIRTHRIGHT LEADERSHIP IN DIVINE PRIESTHOOD

Preservation of Israel's House of Joseph from Absorption by Other Races, a Miracle of History—Joseph's Birthright, Anciently and Now—Latter Day Developments

Early in the year 1841, less than eleven years after the Church of Jesus Christ of Latter-day Saints (frequently referred to as the Mormon Church) was organized, its first President, the Prophet Joseph Smith, was requested to make a brief statement of the belief of his people. This he did in what is now known as the Articles of Faith. Respecting revelation from the Divine Source, he said:

"We believe the Bible to be the word of God, as far as it is translated correctly. We also believe the Book of Mormon to be the word of God. We believe all that God has revealed, all that He does now reveal; and we believe that He will yet reveal many great and important things pertaining to the kingdom of God."

This is a comprehensive statement of Jehovah as Lawgiver and Revealer of heavenly things to humankind; for the guidance of the children of God in their mortal existence. It recognizes the revelations of God to Adam, to Enoch, to Noah, to Abraham, to Moses, and to other worthies named in the old Hebrew Scriptures, and in collateral records. It subscribes to the teachings of Christ and His disciples in the New Testament. It regards the truth that God remembers one nation like unto another, and that the dwellers on the American continent, in both of the great civilizations that existed here and have passed away, had had made known to them the Divine Word. It

also is a declaration that at this time, as well as in the years
to come, the heavens have not "become as brass;" but
that, as in His Providence it becomes necessary, the chan-
nel of revelation from God to man is free and untrammeled.
Its proclamation is of an actual fact, as expressed in one
of the Latter-day Saints' hymns:

> "Jehovah speaks! Let earth give ear!
>   And Gentile nations turn and live.
> His mighty arm is making bare,
>   His covenant people to receive."

It is an announcement, too, that this is the Dispensation of the Fulness of Times; when there shall be gathered
into one all this revealed record, "to the convincing of the
Jew and Gentile that Jesus is the Christ, the Eternal God,
and that the resurrected Jesus of Nazareth, with God His
Father as the first and the Holy Ghost as the third person-
age, constitute the Eternal Godhead of real Christianity—
the Father, Son and Holy Ghost.

Divine Fountain of Truth

*It is not to be understood, from the verse of the hymn
quoted, that the word "Gentile" with its various meanings,
is here applicable only to non-Israel peoples. Its distinction as now made is as between the Jews—descendants
of the two tribes of the "House of Judah"—and all other
nationalities throughout the earth as a unit, whether or
not of Israelitish origin. The completed record of the
revelations from God includes, the account of the resurrected Savior's visit to the Ten Tribes—descendants of
the nationally separate "House of Israel." They were
some of the "other sheep" which were not of the Jews at
Jerusalem.

---

*See questions 12-13, page 195, "God's Covenant Race," Anderson.

This declaration of religious belief in the Divine
Fountain of Truth, and His revelation thereof to man,
embraces all truth in the universe: whether revealed or yet
to be revealed; whether made known through the inspiration of the Almighty that "giveth understanding" to the
spirit of man in his discoveries and developments in the
material things of life; or whether manifest in things visible
or in things invisible to mortal eyes. It embraces every
scientific truth, every historic truth, every truth in philosophy, or logic, or demonstrable fact. That is the scope
of revealed religion. It is the system of law and order
which prevails under heavenly control. It is the Gospel
of the Lord Jesus Christ. It is so-called "Mormonism,"
properly understood.

Man was given a Divine commission to exercise
dominion over the earth. In the exercise of that dominion,
there comes through the intelligence divinely bestowed
upon man much of the heavenly inspiration or revelation
which enables him to utilize the material universe as he
develops in the knowledge of such use. But there is a
higher field of knowledge into which the finite mind cannot venture safely without the direct guidance of that
higher infinite knowledge which comes through regularly
authorized, positive revelation from God. There is a
dominating field of Divine operation in the eternal worlds,
directly affecting the past, the present, the future of mankind, of which finite man can make no physical demon-
stration with his finite knowledge of matter and energy.
That field is the vital, eternal philosophy of life and
destiny in the pre-existent state, in mortality, and in im-
mortality; in the spirit world, the mortal world, and the
resurrected world.

It is no mythical field; it definitely and permanently

exists. In it, the past, the present, and the future, are indestructible facts. Knowledge and understanding thereof come only by direct revelation from the Supreme Ruler who possesses the necessary infinite knowledge. Man as a finite being does not possess it. The revelation thereof to humankind has come from the God of heaven, the God of Abraham, of Isaac, and of Jacob. That revelation is clear and positive, through the voice of God Himself, through the ministry of Jesus of Nazareth who is the Christ of the Living God, and through the prophets whom God has chosen as His mouthpieces as recorded in the history of the world, both ancient and modern. It is the plan of life, of progress, of salvation for mankind. It is known in sacred writ as the Gospel of the Son of God. In its revelation anew in this dispensation through the Prophet Joseph Smith, an outstanding truth in that revelation is Divine "authority to preach the Gospel and administer in the ordinances thereof."

Correct Scriptural Translation

There are people who say that in accepting the Bible as the word of God, the Latter-day Saints, by the clause in the Articles of Faith "as far as it is translated correctly," have a loophole to discard any part of the Authorized Version of the English Bible as not being "correctly translated." Such is not the fact, actual or intended. There is now no difficulty in getting a correct translation on every main point. This was not the case when, in 1841, in justification of some plainer translations in the Book of Mormon, the article of faith quoted was written, all of which harmonize with or explain the Biblical translations. We also have further translations and revisions now which did not exist then.

The actual fact is that in 1841 the Prophet Joseph
Smith was fully justified in applying that saving clause,
and would be so even now. For illustration, take one of
several New Testament passages which have been and
yet are the occasion of much dispute. For instance, here
is one where Bible scholars may agree, but ordinary readers and preachers do not; the masses of the Christian
world are not Bible scholars when it comes to the technical
meaning of either Hebrew or Greek words. The Gospel
of St. Luke, chap. 17, verses 20 and 21, as given in the
King James translation of the Holy Bible, reads:

> "And when He was demanded of the Pharisees, when the
> kingdom of God should come, He answered them and said, The
> kingdom of God cometh not with observation; neither shall they
> say, Lo here, or lo there! for, behold, the kingdom of God is within
> you."

How often do disputants over Bible words, in English, insist that the expression "cometh not with observation" means "a presence wholly invisible to human eyes!"
This is done notwithstanding the explanation given in the
marginal references that it means "with outward show."
The Greek word translated "observation" would be as
correctly rendered "great display." The Pharisees an-
ticipated just that kind of a coming. They were looking
for a splendid deliverance which would throw off the
Roman yoke and give to Judah a world-wide dominion.
Indeed, at the present time, Jews still are looking for
the world-wide dominion formerly hoped for. Great
Britain's promise of Palestine as a homeland for the Jews,
and the aim of Zionism for an independent Jewish government in that land, with the enforced migration of many
Jews thitherward, are looked upon as encouraging steps
toward the attainment of that ambitious aim. It is this
fixed and all-pervading thought in the minds of controlling

forces in Jewry the world over that caused some of the recent disagreements in Palestine. This dominant ambition is the primary motive of non-Christian Jews today in leading nations, not excepting the United States, for seeking collusion in position and wealth in more than a proportionate degree—"to get power and gain," using a scriptural expression—working in the former day by methods of religion and in the latter time by methods economic, yet with the same purpose. Turning now from this picture, and reverting anew to the former conditions, when the Roman power was in control, and its overthrow anxiously, and to them worthily, sought for, its secluded hope then was in the now well known fact that throughout all Palestine—in far away Galilee, in the little villages among the hills, and the busy towns by the lake, down in southern Judea, in the beautiful capital Jerusalem, and in the sacred cities of the priests and elsewhere throughout all Jewry, the whisper was passing from one drooping spirit to another, "Patience! the kingdom of Messiah is at hand."

The Roman yoke was repugnant and heavy. The people were looking for a king of the House of David, greater than David in battle, and more glorious than Solomon in all his glory, to overwhelm their enemies. It was this sort of coming that Jesus told them would not then be. It was not to be with "observation," with "outward show," or with a "great display" that then would startle the world and bring into action the Roman cohorts. Yet there was no suggestion of "invisibility" in the Master's statement. The visible King and visible disciples already were there—actually there, within the gathered concourse to whom Jesus was speaking, yet with no display of human pomp and power.

Further Illustration of Translation

Then, too, how often are discourses preached, how many volumes of discussion have been written and published, endeavoring to convince people that the words "the kingdom of God is within you" mean an internal possession by the individual man or woman—a sort of intestinal emotion! This interpretation of the translation, too, notwithstanding the marginal reference stating that the word "within" there used means "among." The Greek word **entos** translated "within" has no implication of an internal possession of the individual human body— its brain or trunk; it refers to presence in an assembly, or company, or body of people. Right there, in that place, within the assemblage to whom Jesus was speaking, and actually mingling among the Pharisees who were demanding replies to their questions, was the kingdom of God, its authority and power, spiritually, albeit not exercising temporal control of the people. It was there by the presence of the King Himself surrounded by some of His devoted subjects, His faithful disciples. To an actual Bible student the full and correct translation of the sentence would convey the precise idea expressed on this subject by the Prophet Joseph Smith: "There was a legal Administrator, and those that were baptized were subjects for a King; and also the laws and oracles of God were there; therefore the kingdom of God was there."

Thus the very discussions, numerous and sometimes heated, over the verses quoted from St. Luke, definitely justify the care of the Prophet Joseph Smith in stating the Latter-day Saints' belief in the Bible as "the word of God, as far as it is translated correctly," in his comparison with the correct translation in the Book of Mormon. If he had omitted this clause, men could have said he was not inspired as a prophet, otherwise he would have known of translations and revisions yet to come in explanation of translations already made.

Gospel of Establishing Christ's Kingdom

An illustration of divergence in translations now in use, though not such as present a material contradiction in the mind of the careful reader as to the main fact, may be found in that notably important passage now frequently quoted as the fourteenth verse of the twenty-fourth chapter of St. Matthew. The Authorized version reads:

"And this Gospel of the kingdom shall be preached in all the world for a witness unto all nations; and then shall the end come."

The Revised Version and the American Standard Version read:

"And this Gospel of the kingdom shall be preached in the whole world for a testimony unto all the nations; and then shall the end come."

Young's Literal Translation reads:

'And this good news of the reign shall be proclaimed in all the world, for a testimony to all the nations; and then shall the end arrive."

The Twentieth Century New Testament reads:

"And this good news of the kingdom will be proclaimed throughout the world as a testimony to all nations; and then will come the end."

Weymouth's New Testament, which is an effort to use present-day speech, reads:

"And this good news of the kingdom shall be proclaimed throughout the whole world to set the evidence before all the Gentiles; and then the end will come."

Farrer Fenton's Complete Bible in Modern English reads:

"The good news of the kingdom, however, shall be proclaimed throughout the whole empire, as a witness to all nations; and then the end will come."

The translation by the Prophet Joseph Smith reads:

"And again, this Gospel of the kingdom shall be preached in all the world for a witness unto all nations, and then shall the end come, or the destruction of the wicked."

Unifying the idea conveyed in various forms by these translations, a highly interesting and important fact is revealed. The declaration therein is not limited to the preaching of what is commonly termed the Gospel of salvation. That is, the meaning of "the Gospel of the kingdom" is not restricted to St. Paul's mention of "repentance from dead works and of faith toward God, of the doctrine of baptisms, and of laying on of hands, and of resurrection of the dead, and of eternal judgment." It reaches farther, much farther. It is the doctrine of the full establishment of Christ's kingdom on earth, of His millennial reign, when "the earth shall be filled with the knowledge and glory of the Lord, as the waters cover the sea;" when every knee shall bow, and every tongue confess that Jesus Christ is Lord.

The Birthright to Joseph

The Bible has experienced developing translations from the original languages. As early as the fourth century A. D. the translation by Ulfila into Gothic was made; but there was no printing press then, and no known copy exists today. The Vulgate—the authorized Latin translation of the whole Bible—was made by Jerome, 385 to 405 A. D., from the original text, on the basis of an older Latin version called the Itala. Nearly a thousand years later, about 1324 to 1384, the first translation of

the whole Bible into English was made by John Wyclif
and Nicholas Hereford. Then followed Tyndale's, Cov-
erdale's, Matthew's, Taverner's, Cranmer's, the Geneva
version, and the Bishop's Bible, in about the order named.
Next were the two great English translations extant today, the Douai Bible by English Roman Catholic divines,
and King James's translation or the English Authorized
Version by Protestant Christian scholars, out of the original tongues—the Bible used by the Protestant churches
and referred to in the article of faith quoted. These
translations were published in the opening years of the
seventeenth century.

Now, as to these two versions, and churches acting
thereunder. It is said in 1 Chronicles, 5:1, 2:

"The birthright was given unto the sons of Joseph the son of
Israel. . . . For Judah prevailed above his brethren, and of him came
the chief ruler; but the birthright was Joseph's."

The Douai version is that commonly known as the
Roman Catholic Bible, as printed in the English language.
With all its accumulation of tradition, its careful training
of its priesthood, and its commendable discipline in various matters, the Roman Catholic church makes no claim
of lineal descent from Judah, who was given the line of
"chief ruler," including the sceptre of temporal or secular
government exemplified in the royal house of David. This
sceptre to Judah was to continue to the coming of Shiloh—
Prince of Peace—whose mortal descent is of Judah
through David, and who has not yet entered upon the
temporal career of the personally present Messianic kingdom. Nor does the Roman Catholic church pretend to
lineal succession from the Patriarch Jacob's son Joseph,
who, with his sons, had the birthright. In this situation
of actual genealogical descent, therefore, the Romish

church excludes itself from consideration under the statement in the Book of Chronicles. It presents no lineal claim of family descent either to the sceptre or to the birthright.

Quite a different feature appears in that other line which accepts the English Authorized Version as "the word of God" as stated in the article of faith quoted. The birthright was and is in the family of Joseph, with evident Divine design.

Now, as to that birthright fixed in Joseph and his descendants. The Patriarch Abraham took especial care that his son Isaac should not marry a wife "of the daughters of the Canaanites" (Gen. 24:3), but that she should be of the family lineage from which Abraham himself had come. Abraham descended from Noah, through Shem and Eber—the name Hebrew coming from the latter word. The wife of Isaac was to be thoroughly Hebrew, that their children in the family line also should be thoroughly Hebrew. Pharaoh of Egypt "was a partaker of the blood of the Canaanites by birth," "being of that lineage by which he could not have the right of Priesthood" (Book of Abraham 1:27). By that rule Isaac's marriage to a Canaanitish wife would deprive the children of Abraham's divinely-promised son of the lineal birthright to that priesthood—namely the lineal right of leadership or presidency in the ministration of heavenly ordinances and ceremonies. This birthright leadership did not preclude service in the priesthood by others, as for illustration in later years, while "the birthright was Joseph's" (1 Chron. 5:2), descendants of Levi were eligible and selected to service in the priesthood calling. Abraham guarded that lineal birthright heritage with a jealous care; hence designated the family into which his son Isaac should marry.

Dispensation to Abraham

Through his great faith in God, Abraham had received this birthright "from the fathers." He had had his home in the land of the Chaldeans, at the residence of his father who had turned from righteousness to the worship of heathen gods. Abraham was himself a follower of righteousness, and worshiped the true God. He realized that only thereby came the great happiness and peace and rest for which his soul was yearning. His desire for this was so strong, and his conduct in life so different from that of his heathen associations, that the priest of Pharaoh sought to offer him as a human sacrifice to the Egyptian sun-god. Abraham beseeched the heavens for deliverance from heathenism and from the Chaldean heathens. The heavens were opened to his vision. An angel of God's presence freed him; and Jehovah made to him a promise that he should receive the Holy Priesthood which had been held by his ancestor Noah, saying, "through thy ministry My name shall be known in the earth forever, for I am thy God" (Book of Abraham 1:19).

It was a glorious promise, relating to all eternity. The great Patriarch prized its fulfilment beyond the value of his mortal life. It was the aim of his soul, of whose desire the Lord had had foreknowledge. Because of this, upon his being rescued from death at the hands of the heathen priest, the Lord informed him, "Thou wast chosen before thou wast born." In his own words, Abraham tells of his heart's desire for the possession of the birthright:

"I sought for mine appointment unto the Priesthood according to the appointment of God unto the fathers concerning the seed" (Bk. of Abr. 1:4).

This birthright was given to Abraham, who says of himself:

"I became a rightful heir, a high priest, holding the right belonging to the fathers. It was conferred upon me from the fathers. It came down from the fathers, from the beginning of time, yea, even from the beginning, or before the foundations of the earth, to the present time, even the right of the firstborn on the first man, who is Adam, our first father, through the fathers, unto me" (Book of Abraham 1:2-3).

So Abraham obtained the birthright of that leadership in the Priesthood of God. It was the dispensation of the Gospel to Abraham. In modern times we call that Priesthood the Melchizedek Priesthood, out of reverence to the name of the Supreme Being and to avoid too frequent repetition of that name. Abraham cherished it as the pearl of great price in the world's possessions. In this record of his obtaining it is the explanation of his care to have his son Isaac inherit the birthright "concerning the seed." And because of that fact, Rebekah was chosen as Isaac's wife.

Esau's Disregard of Lineage Right

Later came Esau, the firstborn of Isaac and Rebekah. Esau disregarded this lineage. He "despised his birthright." He took a wife of the daughters of the Hittites, which was a "grief of mind unto Isaac and to Rebekah" (Gen. 26:34, 35). Why this grief of mind? The Hittites were Canaanites with whom Isaac had been forbidden to marry. By this marriage of Esau his children would be "partakers of the blood of the Canaanites by birth"— a lineage by which they could not then have right to the Priesthood. It was indeed a cause of "grief of mind" to his parents. By his own action in this marriage, Esau had forfeited the birthright as the firstborn. His lack of re-

gard for the birthright was shown when he sold it to his
brother Jacob to satisfy his hunger. He had lost the
birthright through sin—through violation of the rule necessary to retain it in his children. He was not ignorant of
that fact. Neither was Jacob, as the Bible record shows.
The only other son to receive the birthright was Esau's
younger brother, Jacob, who must himself observe the
necessary rule to retain it.

Then Esau, scheming, wily, and unscrupulous as his
modern descendant the "unspeakable Turk," set about to
gain by deception that which he had forfeited in his posterity, and thus circumvent the Divine purpose of the
birthright in Abraham's family. His father Isaac grew
aged and blind. As the typical Englishman today is a
legendary lover of his "roast beef," so Isaac loved the
savory venison of Esau's chase. By this means of human
appetite, the sinner sought to obtain the blessing which
could no longer be his.

Rebekah's Justification

But his mother was not to be deceived. Like her
relative and father-in-law Abraham, she would guard
with jealous care the birthright in the Abrahamic family.
Scheming had to be met by scheming, as sometimes war
has to be met with war. The American people do not
like war. But a hundred and fifty years ago it was the
only means by which that which we now know as the
United States could be relieved from foreign control. The
life of this nation depended upon it. So it was with Rebekah and Jacob. This good woman, the choice of God for
the mother of Abraham's progeny, matched her skill with
that of her would-be deceiving son, and triumphed. The
birthright was retained in the Abrahamic family, as God

had promised. It came to Jacob's line through his obedience to Divine requirements.

In due process, this birthright came to Joseph and
his descendants, as stated in the Book of Chronicles. It
never was taken away or alienated from them. They
complied with the condition of its inheritance, so far as
their genealogy or blood descent is concerned. Joseph's
wife Asenath was not the daughter of Potiphar, Pharaoh's
Egyptian officer to whom Joseph had been sold by his
brethren. She was of an entirely different family line,
being the daughter of Potipherah, a priest or prince of
On (Gen. 41:45, 50; 46:20), which city was later known
to the Greeks as Heliopolis, where the Obelisk (sometimes
called Cleopatra's needle), now in Central Park, New
York, formerly stood. Therefore, there was in Joseph's
family line none of "the blood of the Canaanites by birth;"
his wife was the daughter of the prince of On, a Shemite
city whose people were idol worshipers as was Abraham's
father Terah and Rachel's father Laban (Gen. 31:19).

As to Joseph's son Ephraim (who was set first by
Jacob), many and just are the criticisms brought against
him for his idolatry and unwisdom. The Prophet Hosea
calls him a half-baked cake: "Ephraim is a cake not
turned." But there never was the accusation that he
forfeited his birthright in the family lineage—a birthright
to be entered upon when his descendants should follow his
father Abraham's example, and seek the "appointment
unto the Priesthood according to the appointment of God
unto the fathers concerning the seed," and should prove
worthy of it by bringing forth the fruits of the kingdom
of God. Ages might pass before that development should
come, but the promise was there. Ephraim still was one
of the Hebrew twelve patriarchs—the inheritors of Is·

rael's blessing.   More than a thousand years after the
conferring of the blessing by Jacob, the Prophet Jeremiah
makes this record:

"For thus saith the Lord. . . . I am a father to Israel, and Ephraim
is my firstborn" (Jer. 31:7, 9).

Inheritance by Joseph's Line

So "the birthright was Joseph's" and in his family.
Jehovah's name was not to be known through the ministry
of Abram, Ishmael, and Esau.   It is the God of Abraham,
of Isaac, and of Jacob, "in the earth forever."

The Bible gives the record of many precious promises
made to Joseph and his descendants (Gen. 49:22-26; Deut.
33:13-17).

It is Joseph who is to "push the people together to
the ends of the earth."

Joseph, of whom the Lord said, "Blessed be the land"
for the precious things of the heavens, of the earth, and
of the seas.

Joseph, who should have dominion in the precious
fruits brought forth by the sun, and put forth by the moon.

Joseph, who was to control the chief things of the
ancient mountains and the everlasting hills.

Joseph, who should have the precious things of the
earth and the fulness thereof.

Joseph, who was to be a fruitful bough by a deep
water.

Joseph, whose branches should "run over the wall" to
the utmost bound of the everlasting hills.

Joseph, whom the archers would sorely grieve, and
shoot at, and hate.

Joseph, whose bow was to abide in strength, and

whose hands were to be made strong by the hands of the mighty God of Jacob.

Joseph, whom God would help, and whom the Almighty would bless.

Joseph, whose descendants should be the ten thousands of Ephraim and the thousands of Manasseh in multitude.

Joseph, whose "horns" were to be as "the horns of the unicorns" in their strength, and whose glory is as "the firstling of his bullock."

Joseph, who was to have "the good will of Him that dwelt in the bush" and who had declared of Himself, "I am the God of thy father, the God of Abraham, the God of Isaac, and the God of Jacob."

All these and more are the blessings which the Bible declares "shall be on the head of Joseph, and on the crown of him that was separate from his brethren." It is the most marvelous, the most glorious promise ever pledged to any race or family among earth's inhabitants. Only God could make safely such a promise; and only God could keep it.

Israel's Division into Judah and Ephraim

At the death of King Solomon, the Israelites became separated into two nations. The prophets refer to them frequently as the "House of Judah" and the "House of Israel." The "House of Israel" is also named Ephraim, after its leading tribe. The name "House of Isaac" also is applied to it (Amos 7:16): "In Isaac shall thy seed be called" (Gen. 21:12; Rom. 9:7; Heb. 11:18). Its membership is "Joseph and all the house of Israel his companions;" while the house of Judah comprises "Judah and the children of Israel his companions." They were the ten-tribed nation and the two-tribed nation.   The two-tribed nation, although denationalized and scattered, never has been lost in the sense of being known as Jews and recognized everywhere.   The ten-tribed nation turned to the worship of other gods.   Ephraim-Israel was "joined to his idols."   Carried away captive, ultimately they lost the name of Israel, and of Joseph, and of Ephraim.   Jehovah declared of them: "Ye are not my people, and I will not be your God" (Hosea 1:9).

Thus the "birthright" nation became lost to the knowledge of the world, even to their brethren the Jews.   They were "lost sheep of the house of Israel."   Purely Gentile or non-covenant peoples are never termed "sheep" in the Bible.   That term is applied there only to the chosen Abrahamic race.   The record says they went to the north.   The "north countries" as we know them geographically today are northern Europe, northern Asia, and northern America.   The historian Josephus, writing near the close of the first century, 95 A.D., says:

"There are but two tribes in Asia and Europe subject to the Romans, while the ten tribes are beyond the Euphrates till now, and are an immense multitude, not to be estimated by numbers."

This statement does not identify them by different tribal names, or by the name they may have borne at that time.   In that sense, their location by Josephus is indefinite.   But the fact of their being numerous is clear.   The eminent Jewish scholar Isaac Leeser, who translated the Hebrew Scriptures for the English-speaking Jews, says in his great work "The Jewish Religion:"

"Let us observe that by this return of the captives (the Jews from Babylon) the Israelitish nation was not restored; since the ten tribes, who had formerly composed the kingdom of Israel, were yet left in banishment; and to this day the researches of travelers and wise men have never been able to trace their fate."

House of Judah Not All of Israel, and Not the House of Israel Nation

Nor is this all. For many years a gross fiction has been imposed upon the civilized world by religious and secular teachers and authors. In commentaries and histories, in universities, colleges, and theological seminaries, in religious and secular newspapers, by lecturers, doctors of divinity and church dignitaries, the people have been told that all Israelites are Jews. A common definition for the word "Jews" is, "A name given to all the descendants of Abraham," or, "A name given to the descendants of Abraham, who were divided into twelve tribes."

The well-known English Orientalist, Sir H. C. Rawlinson, writing of the ten-tribed kingdom of Israel, says: "They ceased to exist." S. Baring-Gould, English divine and man of letters, and others, tell us that "God's first purpose has been partially frustrated. The church has taken Israel's place as the body. One commentator who is frequently quoted says: "The ten tribes were not lost, but simply lost their tribehood and returned to Palestine not as organized tribes but as individuals. Hence all this hue and cry about the lost tribes, ransacking all the world to find them, and writing vast volumes, is a piece of twaddle and nonsense." The encyclopedias have similar misleading statements. The Encyclopedia Britannica says: "The exiled Israelites were absorbed by the surrounding heathenism without leaving a trace behind them."

Little wonder that, under the thought that all existing Israelites are Jews, some men of note turned against the Bible. Of these, Thomas Paine asserts that he was led into infidelity because he saw that the Jewish people never had and never could fulfil the prophecies of the Old Testament. The noted Rationalist, Charles Bradlaugh, deal ing with the same idea, declared, "You tell me that the God of the Bible always speaks the truth! I do not believe it!" The one-time great evangelist B. Ray Mills turned from the Bible for the same reason, saying: "The prophecies of the Old Testament to Israel have not been realized. Today, the Bible is no more inspired than the Koran." This error respecting the existence of ten-tribed Israel prevailed in all the Christian world at the opening of the nineteenth century. Truly, "teaching for doctrine the commandments of men" is "an abomination" to the Lord!

Bulk of the Israelites Not Jews

Yet the Jews are Israelites; but they are only two of the twelve tribes of the chosen Abrahamic race. The great bulk of the Israelites are not Jews, any more than the great bulk of Americans are New Englanders; yet the New Englanders are Americans. The Bible prophecies and promises to the "House of Joseph," or "Ephraim," or "House of Israel" apart from the "House of Judah," were not for the Jews at all, but for that other branch of Israel, the "birthright" division; and in them must the fulfilment be looked for. A recent writer who has grasped the situation says: "In writing the history of Israel we must needs write the history of the Jews, but we could write the history of the Jews and not write the history of Israel."

Thus the entire Christian world was in a dilemma at the opening of the nineteenth century, owing to this gross fiction. If they believed the Bible prophecies and promises relative to the "House of Joseph" or Ephraim-Israel branch were possible of fulfilment, the only way out of the dilemma that could give them understanding was

direct revelation from God. The Bible did not contain
the direct and positive information, though in it was recorded the promises of which this is a type:

> "I will strengthen the House of Judah, and I will save the
> House of Joseph, and I will bring them again to place them; for I
> have mercy upon them; and they shall be as though I had not cast
> them off: for I am the Lord their God, and will hear them. And
> Ephraim shall be like a mighty man, and their heart shall rejoice"
> (Zach. 10:6, 7).
> "Moreover, I will make a covenant of peace with them; it shall
> be an everlasting covenant with them; and I will place them, and
> multiply them, and will set my sanctuary in the midst of them
> forevermore. My tabernacle also shall be with them: yea, I will
> be their God, and they shall be My people" (Ezek. 37:26, 27).

Preservation of Israel's House of Joseph

The segregation of the Jews from other races while
mingling with them has been termed a miracle of history.
But the segregation of the House of Joseph part of the
Abrahamic race from absorption by other races while
mingling with them, and the fulfilment of the blessings
placed on the head of Joseph, thus making world leaders
of this branch of Israel, is a far more wonderful miracle,
in view of their racial identity having been hidden for
more than two thousand years. In other words, the pres-
ervation of Israel's House of Joseph from absorption by
other races is indeed a miracle of history. "The birthright was Joseph's," and without his branch of Israel
there could be no fulfilment. Only through revelation
from God could the identity of Joseph's descendants be
made known positively, and the blessings of the birthright
tribe come to them. The Ephraim tribe, leader of the
ten tribes, must be the actual, lineal, blood descent of
Joseph and his sons to claim the birthright; and only Jehovah knew the fact in the circumstances, and could reveal
the same. In no other way but by this revelation could

the Bible be maintained in this respect as "the word of God." From all the other features of Bible information, and from the approaching culmination of world affairs, the time was at hand, at the beginning of the nineteenth century, for that revelation. It must come soon, or fail; and the works of God fail not.

Now for the modern history. Did the revelation come, and how? It was in the spring of 1820 A.D. that a youth living in the western part of the State of New York, imbued with unshaken faith in the Bible and the promises of God, read in the Epistle of James "to the twelve tribes which are scattered abroad"—not to the two-tribed Jews, but "to the twelve tribes:"

"If any of you lack wisdom, let him ask of God, that giveth to all men liberally, and upbraideth not; and it shall be given him."

This youth, Joseph Smith, then fourteen years of age, said that in answer to his prayer he received a glorious heavenly vision. In line with that manifestation, seven years later he was entrusted with the translation, by the gift and power of God, of a sacred record of ancient inhabitants of America. Its doctrines, its testimony, its prophecies, were in strict accord with the same features in the Bible. It revealed a people whose progenitor had come to America from Palestine, and who said he was of the tribe of Manasseh, which tribe had been assigned to the nation Ephraim (1 Kings 11:31, 32, 35; 12:20-23; 2 Chron. 11:1-6; 30:11; Ekez. 37:16-19). This youth had no knowledge at that time, or opportunity for such knowledge, that he was himself a lineal, blood descendant of that Patriarch Jacob's son Joseph to whom had been given the birthright; and that he, Joseph Smith, was an actual inheritor of that birthright. It was a revelation from God to him, as thus told in the record:

"Joseph (who was carried into Egypt) truly testified, saying: A seer shall the Lord my God raise up, who shall be a choice seer unto the fruit of my loins. Yea, Joseph truly said: Thus saith the Lord unto me: A choice seer will I raise up out of the fruit of thy loins; and he shall be esteemed highly among the fruit of thy loins. And unto him will I give commandment that he shall do a work for the fruit of thy loins, his brethren, which shall be of great worth unto them, even to the bringing of them to the knowledge of the covenants which I have made with thy fathers. . . . And his name shall be called after me; and it shall be after the name of his father. And he shall be like unto me; for the thing which the Lord shall bring forth by his hand, by the power of the Lord shall bring my people unto salvation." (2 Nephi 3:6, 7, 15).

Revealing the Ten-Tribed Israel Nation

It was also the revelation from God of the existence among men of the "House of Joseph," or the ten-tribed nation Ephraim, in latter days—the opening view of this miracle of history. It was the word of God, coming from the Book of Mormon, where that item of history had been preserved. The "choice seer" was Joseph the Prophet. He was called, and in due time ordained. He was inspired for the mission of the birthright seed. He received the dispensation of the Gospel of Abraham. He received the keys of the gathering of Israel, and of leading the lost Ten Tribes—an inheritance from his progenitor Joseph who had the "birthright" (Doc. and Cov. 110:11). He received the keys of the Gospel of Christ for the salvation of the living and the dead. It was the birthright of Israel. Those who believed in the divinity of his message proclaimed, "Now is the day of Israel." They sang of "Ephraim crowned with his blessings in Zion." They joined in the hymn which has been carried to every Anglo-Saxon people in the world:

"Israel, Israel! God is calling,
　Calling thee from lands of woe.
Babylon the great is falling—
　God will all its towers o'erthrow.
Come to Zion! Come to Zion
　Ere His floods of anger flow.

"Israel, Israel! Canst thou linger
    Still in error's gloomy ways?
Mark how judgment's pointing finger
    Justifies no vain delays.
Come to Zion! Come to Zion!
    Zion's walls shall ring with praise."

Without this revelation from God, Joseph Smith could know nothing then of the continued existence of the Ten Tribes. Neither history nor genealogy at that time furnished him anything definite; from these he could not learn of his own lineage, or of any lineage outside of Judah. The word of God in the Book of Mormon gave him the information. It also told him that long-lost Israel or the Ten Tribes, "are scattered to and fro upon the isles of the sea" (1 Nephi 22:4); and that "great are the promises of the Lord unto those who are upon the isles of the sea" (2 Nephi 10:21). This revelation from God was necessary not only for Joseph-Ephraim-Israel, but for all the world; and in the due time of the Lord it was given, with the other revelations and blessings necessary for the organization and mission of the Church of Jesus Christ of Latter-day Saints in this dispensation—"the only true and living Church upon the face of the whole earth" (Doc. and Cov. 1:30).

Birthright by Lineal Descent to Joseph
the Latter-day Prophet

That Church makes no claim of lineal descent from Judah in the latter's role of temporal government through the royal house of David. But in its membership and patriarchal blessings it does assert lineal descent—actual genealogical, family descent—in succession from the Patriarch Jacob's son Joseph, who, with his sons, had the birthright. That Church, therefore—and, by the way, it is the only church presenting such claim—comes directly within the statement of the Book of Chronicles: "the birth-right was Joseph's."   In its Articles of Faith the Prophet Joseph says:

"We believe in the literal gathering of Israel and in the restoration of the Ten Tribes."

That gathering and restoration were to be as stated in the Scriptures.   As early as 1832, the Prophet Joseph Smith openly taught "the return of the lost tribes" to the knowledge and recognition of the world.   It was then a new and strange doctrine to every division of so-called Christianity, and was met with ridicule and antagonism. In 1837, the message to and revelation of Israel crossed the Atlantic to the mother-nation of English-speaking America—to a nation in which faith in the divinity of Jesus Christ had taken deep and lasting root; the nation which had given to the civilized world the English Au-thorized Version of the Bible.

The bearers of that message, humble Elders of Is-rael, endowed with divine authority "to preach the Gospel and administer in the ordinances thereof," taught that Gospel.   They were listened to by many eager souls to whom the Spirit of God bore witness of the truth.   They sang the songs of Latter-day Israel, in their humility doubtless scarce realizing the majesty of the message they were delivering.

But the word "Israel" bore fruit.   "God moves in a mysterious way, His wonders to perform."   The thought that here was a latter-day Prophet whose lineage had been divinely revealed as of that Joseph who held Israel's birthright was startling in itself. It evoked hostility. These messengers from America, the "land of Joseph"—these

"Yankee preachers" they were called then—said the blood
of Ephraim, that branch of Israel distinguished from Judah, would be found in Great Britain and in other northern
countries of Europe! Even their Prophet was the son of
an English father and a Scottish mother! "Preposterous!" said the people who were imbued with the fiction
that all Israelites were Jews. It was reported that in
America those of the British people who received the word
of God through patriarchal blessings were of Joseph and
of Ephraim. "Still more preposterous!" said sectarian
preachers.

Men in Britain who delved into history began to
investigate. At first it was with the idea of disproving
the alleged "preposterous theory" of Ephraim-Israel being
found in the Anglo-Saxon race. Mr. Wilson, an English
historian, investigated. Soon he forgot all about the
"Yankee preachers." He discovered what to his mind
were many evidences, historic and prophetic, of Israel in
the British Isles—the "isles afar off" of the Prophet Isaiah.
He was followed by another English historian, Mr. Glover,
and others, who added to the store of evidence. Sharon
Turner, in his great "History of the Anglo-Saxon Race,"
brought still more testimony. The "Yankee preachers"
were right on this point. The Book of Mormon was "the
word of God" on this point, as were also the revelations
relating thereto promulgated by the Prophet Joseph Smith.
In words the searchers who unearthed this evidence might
not admit that fact, but their discoveries proclaimed it
beyond dispute. Their works are trumpet-tones to the
world. God had revealed a great truth to mankind, and
human research was bringing proofs from historic human
testimony. The article of faith says:

"We believe the Bible to be the word of God, as far as it is translated correctly. We also believe the Book of Mormon to be the word of God. We believe all that God has revealed, all that He does now reveal; and we believe that He will yet reveal many great and important things pertaining to the kingdom of God."

The great Psalmist sang nearly thirty centuries ago: "Behold, He that keepeth Israel shall neither slumber nor sleep" (Psalms 121:4). And He does not, even among men, particularly among those in the chosen race. To-day a vast organization, with a membership of millions reaching into every English-speaking nation and colony on the globe—The British-Israel World Federation, in Great Britain and the Anglo-Saxon Federation of America in the United States—is earnestly and intelligently uphold-ing that which was "preposterous" in the "Yankee preachers" of a hundred years ago, and is making claims going farther, much farther, than those then set forth. These people are basing their claims on the fulfilment of Bible prophecy in history and on the English Bible as "the word of God." The Prophet Hosea (1:9) said God would disown the ten-tribed nation, and these lost the name Israel. But he also prophesied that "in the place" where they had lost that name He would restore it to them; and that with the "children of Judah" they should again be called "children of Israel" (Hosea 1:10, 11).

All this is but a part of the many collateral testimon-ies to the Bible, the Book of Mormon, the revelations through the Prophet Joseph Smith, and the revelations he named as yet to come, as "the word of God." Throughout all Anglo-Saxondom, evidently without a full conscious-ness thereof on the part of men, are being gathered and promulgated volumes of indisputable testimony to the divine mission of the Prophets of God, including Joseph Smith and of his successors in the Church of Jesus Christ of Latter-day Saints.

Contrast in Bible System and Present World System

*For example, the Bible-believing Anglo-Saxon magazine, "Destiny," says of the divine statutes for Israel in contrast with the economic system of today:

"The economic law of the Lord declares every seven years shall be a release for the poor; we have circumvented its operation and are oppressing the needy.

"The law declares, Thou shalt take no usury; we call it interest and collect tribute from our brother.

"The law says, Thou shalt not steal; we legalize great corporations to prey upon our people and rob them of their earnings.

"The law says, The land shall not be sold; we have made it a part of capital and the people have been evicted.

"The law says taxes shall be one-tenth of the increase; we have laid a burden upon the poor which is confiscation of property.

"The law says the rich shall bear the burden of government; we have created tax-exempt investments that they may escape.

"The law says, Remember the Sabbath Day to keep it holy; our people are violating this law while our legislatures have legalized its desecration.

"The law says the poor and the rich shall be treated alike; we have made possession of money the criterion of value so the rich escape while the poor suffer in judgment.

"The law says, Thou shalt not oppress a hired servant; those controlling capital, and the tools of production, are grinding their help for profit."

This is a scorching indictment; but it is the way that Bible-believers among the masses look at it, from the viewpoint of the law of the Lord to Israel anciently. They say that only by a correction of our economic system to comply with the Israel law can peace and prosperity come to the nations.

These investigators have made a survey of the instruction given to young people in Christian Sunday Schools throughout the United States, and here is their finding:

"Having accepted the dictum of the theologians, nine-tenths of the Bible has become a closed book, and the law of the Lord is forgotten. These leaders, like a man lost in the woods, are traveling

*See pages 272 to 291, "God's Covenant Race."—Anderson.

in a circle and leading the people with them. To those who deny this fact, let them read the great volume of literature as represented in the Sunday School lesson outlines of the past decade or two. These purport to be the acme of instruction in Biblical knowledge; yet in what a narrowing circle these so-called teachers have trod! These lessons contain practically nothing of prophecy; nothing of the scope of the law of the Lord; nothing of Jehovah's administration in the affairs of the nation; nothing of the history and prophecy of Israel as distinct from that of Judah; nothing of the certainty of the fulfilment of God's solemn covenant; very few have ever mentioned the second coming as an imminent fact in the life of His Church; neither has instruction been given in the signs, or in the times, so emphasized by our Lord; nor are the people taught the meaning of the restitution of all things which God hath spoken by the mouth of all His holy prophets since the world began. Blind leaders of the blind! It is the Prophet Isaiah (9:16) who says, 'The leaders of this people cause them to err; and they that are led of them are destroyed."

This arraignment for the so-called Christian teaching of today, severe as it may seem, is not to be brushed aside as by extremists or the representatives of any particular cult. It is by experienced, thoughtful, conservative people, in different avenues of life, yet well informed in matters of finance, religious training and industry.

It is reported that recently some one asked George Bernard Shaw whether or not he considered Christianity had been a failure. "Failure!" he exclaimed. "Why not try it?" Food for serious thought comes in the suggestion.

Referring again to the "birthright" of Joseph who was sold into Egypt—coming from his ancestor Abraham and his progenitors—that "birthright" of right to leadership in the Priesthood of God, is in effective operation today, both in the visible and in the invisible world. The possessor of that birthright may, and does and will, have "the archers" shoot at and "sorely grieve" him; but his bow will abide "in strength, and his hands will be made strong by the hands of the mighty God of Jacob." It is the blessing upon the "birthright" son Joseph and upon his descendants who are followers of righteousness.

These combined events foreshadow the "coming of the end" named in the fourteenth verse of the twenty-fourth chapter of St. Matthew's Gospel. The ushering in of Christ's millennial reign approaches. Unbelief will not stay it. Ridicule and enmity will not postpone it. Jehovah's decree is that it is "near at hand."

> "The tide of time is ebbing low;
>   The wheels of change roll fast.
> Hark! the heralds of salvation blow
>   The Gospel trump's loud blast.
> Our God, the source of life and love,
>   To earth His care extends:
> Reveals His word; the host above
>   In holy union blends.
> Awake! Awake! Let the nations hear
>   Jehovah's firm decree
> To abolish sin, and usher in
>   The world's great Jubilee!"

"Blessed are all they which hunger and thirst after righteousness: for they shall be filled with the Holy Ghost," and shall "stand in holy places and not be moved until the day of the Lord come." Amen.

Some Study Questions

1. Repeat from memory the statement in our Articles of Faith respecting revelation from the Divine Source.

2. What do you think of the comprehensiveness of this statement?

3. Can you justify the conditional clause regarding the Bible translation? Give an example.

4. Why is it so important to understand the term "gentiles"* in the Scriptures is sometimes used in a "national sense" meaning everyone including Israelites excepting the Jews or Nephites; and sometimes in the strictly "racial sense" meaning the actual descendants of Japheth. (The Latin and many of the Slavonic races.)

5. What interesting and important fact is discovered by a comparative study of Matt. 24:14.

6. Relate something regarding the various translations of the Bible. Which two are most commonly used?

7. What great promise was made by God to Abraham?

*For examples see I Nephi 13:42 and III Nephi 15:22-23.

8. Are most of the members of our Church today as earnest in their desire to obtain the priesthood as Abraham was? Give reasons for your opinion.

9. Discuss the fact that it was Esau and not Jacob (as is commonly supposed) who tried to steal the birthright.

10. Why was Rebecca justified in taking a hand in this dispute?

11. What were some of the precious promises made to our father Joseph?

12. Are all Israelites Jews? Are all Jews Israelites?

13. How and when was the existence of a lawful heir in this day to the Priesthood birthright leadership of all Israel revealed?

14. In what way is historical research proving the truth of this revelation?

15. Discuss the value and importance to all Latter-day Saints of a proper understanding of the Lord's statement regarding them in the Doctrine and Covenants, Sec. 86:8-11.

"**Thus saith the Lord unto you with whom the Priesthood hath continued through the lineage of your fathers— For ye are lawful heirs according to the flesh** and have been hid from the world with Christ in God. Therefore your life and the Priesthood hath remained and must needs remain through you and your lineage until the restoration of all things spoken by the mouths of all the Holy prophets since the world began. Therefore, blessed are ye if ye continue in my goodness, a light unto the Gentiles, **and through this Priesthood a savior unto my people Israel.** The Lord hath said it. Amen."

SECTION 3

"IN THE MOUTH OF TWO OR THREE WITNESSES SHALL ALL THINGS BE ESTABLISHED."

For this reason we now bring up additional evidence from our third witness to the great Israel story, the Prophet Joseph Smith. In doing so we quote almost exclusively from "The Life of the Prophet Joseph," by Edward W. Tullidge, published in 1878. We should bear in mind that his volume carries a remarkable endorsement in its preface:

"In its compilation I have been placed under obligations to the Hon. Joseph F. Smith and Eliza R. Snow, (the Prophet's wife) who kindly read and revised the manuscript.

"The late President Young requested me to write this book, and the late Apostle George A. Smith, on his death-bed, charged me solemnly concerning it."

Quoted herewith are most of chapters 31, 32 and 33 found on pages 364 through 385.

"And what of the Destiny of Israel in the world's future? Shall the earth have joy and Israel be left desolate? Shall the culmination and crowning of all civilizations come to pass in these latter days, and Jehovah's covenant people have no lot nor part in the matter? . . .

"Will Jehovah answer?

"Nay, hath he not answered in his wondrous dealings with his chosen people?

"In the light of the mission and themes of the Prophet of Latter-day Israel a new and significant interpretation

is given to the curse and "Israel under the curse" becomes a manifestation of Providential manipulation, as
exact in its purposes and outcome as are the methods and
conclusions of a scientific proposition . . .

"We have seen (Section 1 and 2) that civilization
had been moving westward from the beginning of time.
And the learned Moses knew this, for he made the map of
Israel's course and destiny with as much scientific exacti-
tude as an astronomer's sketch of the heavens.

"Had Jacob remained in Palestine he would have
died and been forever entombed there. But such was not
to be his destiny. Israel is Jehovah's living monument,—
by his migrations pointing the very course, and time, and
place of Messiah's coming.

"To the West, by the rod of his providence, has
Jehovah driven his stubborn, self-willed people, to their
greater destiny of the latter-days. And wherever their
affections and fidelities have made them to linger, there
has the rod of his chastisement descended, now in this
guise, now in that, scourging them onward to their Zion,
their blessing, their rest.

"And this accomplished, behold the promise, 'And
he will do thee good and multiply thee above thy fathers.'

"Had Israel, as a nation, understood as much of the
purposes of Jehovah as did Moses and the seers, then had
they been led, not driven, to their destiny. Had Jehovah
succeeded in making of his Israel a nation of prophets and
seers, then had they been taught of him the mystery of
his providence, and the course which the Lord of the
earth was taking, and they would have followed him even
more willingly than when, as the angel of their covenant,
he led them up out of the land of Egypt.

"But with the very promise of their possession of a land flowing with milk and honey came the affirmation that they should leave it at some future time. While it remained thus productive and delightful, and while the East was the center of civilization, they had there a destiny. But by and by Palestine was to become a desert, and by and by the mighty Orient was to become as the sepulchre of empires and civilizations. What business had Israel there in such a day? True, it should come to pass that Jacob should mourn the fall of Jerusalem with an awful lamentation, but above it all might have been heard the voice of Jehovah: 'Let the dead bury the dead: follow me!'

"Had Israel been wise unto salvation, the chosen people had not sat so long under the shadow of impending doom. Had he hearkened unto the Lord before the day of that doom's appearing, then had he understood the thunderings of impending calamities to have been the self-same voice that spake to Abraham, 'Get thee out of thy country, and from thy kindred, and from thy father's house, unto a land that I will show thee.'

"And was not this exactly the case with Lehi and his little Israelitish colony, who left Jerusalem in the days of Zedekiah, — just in time to escape the awful scourge of Nebuchadnezzar, — giving the initial subject of the Book of Mormon?

"Furthermore, did not the Jehovah-fearing men of England (in the seventeenth century, after the star of Bethlehem had risen to pilot the shepherds westward) hear this same command, 'Get thee out of thy country? . . .

"These of England, in the seventeenth century, were a better Israel than they of old. And out of their obedience and true Israelitish faith an empire has already grown up in America, mightier and more blessed than all the empires of the past, — a kingdom without a king, waiting Messiah's coming. . . .

"And so all Israel shall be saved: as it is written, There shall come out of Zion the Deliverer, and he shall turn away ungodliness from Jacob."

"And this is the significance of the rise of Joseph of the West, whose mission is the prophecy of the Deliverer that shall come out of this Zion of all the earth.

"But ye shall be named the Priests of the Lord: men shall call you the ministers of our God: ye shall eat the riches of the Gentiles, and in their glory shall ye boast yourselves. * * *

"And their seed shall be known among the Gentiles, and their offspring among the people: all that see them shall acknowledge them, that they are the seed which the Lord hath blessed. * * *

"For as the earth bringeth forth her bud, and as the garden causeth the things that are sown in it to spring forth; so the Lord God will cause righteousness and praise to spring forth before all the nations.   (Isaiah 61:6,9 -11)

"Judah has been well defined among the nations, by the curse which has scarred his brow; but here is described an Israel which shall be known for the blessing, not the curse.

"Much light is thrown upon this point by the enlarged views of Joseph (Smith). According to his finding, Jacob and his children are empires. The great Germanic race is the seed of Ephraim, or at least the seed of Ephraim is very markedly mixed in that race. The Scandinavian peoples are also greatly of Ephraim; and so, as matter of course, are the English and American nations.

In this view of Israel let us now read the promise made to Abraham, by Jehovah, who "keepeth covenants:

"Behold my covenant is with thee, and thou shalt be a father of many nations. * * * I will make nations of thee, and kings shall come out of thee.

"And to Sarah: 'I will bless her, and she shall be a mother of nations; kings of people shall be of her.'

"Surely this had a fulfillment beyond that of the Israel in Palestine, with the short record of his kings,—so insignificant that the mighty rulers of the heathen scorned to recognize them.

"With this splendid view of Israel which Joseph has given, it can be easily imagined that some of the most potent monarchs of Europe have been of Israelitish blood, and that the mightiest spirits that have moved the world for the last thousand years were the offspring of men such as were known of old as Jehovah's prophets.

"This gives new light indeed to the whole history of Christendom. Abraham is a 'father of nations;' 'kings of people' have come of him.

"And here may be presented the singular fact that Great Britain bears the arms of Israel, — the lion of Judah and the unicorn of Ephraim.

" 'Judah is a lion's whelp.' Messiah himself is called the 'Lion of the Tribe of Judah.' Of Joseph, Moses said: 'His glory is like the firstling of his bullock, and his horns are like the horns of unicorns; with them he shall push the people together to the ends of the earth: and they are the ten thousands of Ephraim, and they are the thousands of Manasseh." '

"The royal arms of Great Britain should therefore ethnologically signify a mixture of the blood of David and the blood of Joseph. The Welsh people show much of this Hebrew element in them. David is almost a national name among them. The Welsh harp is also suggestive of the Psalmist King.

"And now let us historically test this Israelitish subject, as enlarged by Joseph. Let the text be 'Their seed shall be known among the Gentiles.'

"The blood of Israel will be known by its manifestations. The Israelitish genius will speak in the peoples who are of Israel. This may be made quite a scientific problem.

"And Israel will most certainly antagonize the Romish power. The genius of Judah and the genius of Rome can but be in deadly antipathy. Rome was that 'nation of fierce countenance' that destroyed Jerusalem. And who destroyed the Roman Empire? Israel! — The Ephraimites!

"In the third and fourth centuries of the Christian era the Germanic hosts poured down resistlessly upon the iron empire of the Caesars, and upon its ruins built the empires of the West. In Ephraim was Jehovah's vengeance upon that nation of fierce countenance, that destroyed his once beloved Jerusalem.

"Alfred, the founder of England's greatness, was strangely Israelitish in character and method; and his writings, which are voluminous, are peculiarly like those of David and Solomon.

"But it is to the period of the Protestant Reformation, and that of the Cromwellian Revolution, that we must go for the most strictly Israelitish manifestations. In those days the God of Jacob was not confounded.

"First arose John de Wickcliffe. He was called "The Morning Star of the Reformation.' That star rose in England then, just as in this age it could rise only in America; for the star of both empire and reformation had crossed the Atlantic.

"Wickliffe's controversy struck direct at Rome, else had he been no morning star of Israel. He it was who called the Pope 'Antichrist,' and spake of him as 'the proud worldy priest of Rome, — the most cursed of clippers and purse-kervers (cut-purses).' He it was who translated and unsealed the Hebrew Scriptures. And thus was it England's destiny to open the seals of Judah's Book. From that hour, as from an archangel's trump, rang forth the doom of the Romish Church. But what shall the awful pronouncement be when Judah himself sends back upon Rome the curse of ages?

"A century and a half later, in Germany, Luther arose, and burned the bull of the Pope. Rome had a terrible fall over the Germanic nation. Those Ephraimites proved their blood.

"At about this time, however, Charles V., of Germany and Spain, attempted to restore the universal power of Rome to more than its pristine glory, while his brother-in law, Henry VIII, of England, threw his might of character into the same scale. Fateful days for Israel! Will Jehovah fail him?

"A woman for the sacrifice! One in whose veins flows the sacred blood! Anne Boleyn! The issue lost her head, but it cost Rome a world!

"From her Elizabeth! Born on the eve of the Virgin's nativity! Died on the eve of the Virgin's annunciation! The 'Virgin Queen,' indeed!

"Surely here is Hebrew mystery! Surely here is a star of the house of David risen in the West!

"And statesmen, as well as mystics, were influenced by the sign of her imperial mission. In her was the fate of the world. With might and majesty she threw herself into the trembling balance, becoming the very prophetess and saviour of Protestantism. Calling herself the Lioness of England, she became in fact the Lioness of the Lord, and fulfilled a truly divine mission as the head of the English Church. The bishops of the Romish Church refused to crown her, and in her lifetime three Popes excommunicated her, but she forced her crowning and anointing, and in three months after her ascension overturned the entire Romish hierarchy throughout her realm. When the Pope anathematized her she ordered an anathema to be hurled back in his teeth from the solemn portals of St. Paul, a proceeding without precedent, and which probably no other mortal in Christendom would have dared to do. And when finally Pope Sextus and all the Catholic princes of Europe joined in a crusade against her, a mighty storm destroyed their invincible Armada off the English Coast. In those days 'twas said, 'The Lord did it.' Whatever may be said today, there never were such examples since the word began, till Cromwell and his Jehovah-fearing men cut off the head of their king in the name of the Lord of Hosts.

"The England of Cromwell's day was as Israelitish as were the tribes of Jacob when David reigned in Jerusalem.

"But at this date already had New England arisen. The Pilgrims had landed on Plymouth Rock, and Israel was migrating toward the Zion of the latter-days. The setting up of Messiah's kingdom was now a prophecy well defined; the voice of the age was crying, 'The Kingdom of Heaven is at hand.'

"And what a remarkable fact is it that Israel in the seventeenth century actually attempted to establish the Zion of the Lord in England! That which those God-fearring men of the Commonwealth undertook was no political revolution, in the ordinary sense; it was an Israelitish upheaval in the world, — an upheaval that was sure to repeat itself in America.

"And those men of God, in the seventeenth century, called themselves 'The Saints,' and 'The Latter-day Israel,' just as do the Saints of America in the nineteenth century. Neither of them have minced their language in this regard. Indeed, they speak in the same tongue, the same words: their themes are one. The Latter-day Saints of England, under Cromwell, and these Latter-day Saints of America, under Joseph Smith, are the only two peoples who have strictly resembled each other during the whole Christian era. And the crowning fact is that not only do both possess the same genius, but one is literally the offspring of the other.

"For a full century Israel, among the nations, was actually proving his blood. Notably so in Germany, England, the Netherlands, and Scandinavia.

"What then shall we say of these wondrous manifestaions of an Israel among the nations, — the voice of his genius and the instincts of his blood? Is all this but the noise of Jehovah's chariots passing by? Are not his angels turning earthward? Is there no purpose in this tumult of his coming?

"And finally, let us mark the fact that the foundations of our American nationality were not laid by Godless and ambitious colonists, but by the very men who had already raised in England the standard of Messiah. Then came the Revolution under Washington, and the mighty Republic emerged upon the theatre of nations. At last a magnificent kingdom, without a king, — the Zion of God awaiting the coming her Lord! Then came Joseph, crying in the ears of men, 'Behold the kingdom of heaven is at hand!'

"But the churches were deaf to this prophet of glorious tidings; therefore have they sealed their own doom. They shall pass away. Rejecting Messiah, in their rejection of His Prophet, they shall themselves be rejected of Him at his coming.

"Yet will Israel prevail, for outside of churches is gathering a mighty host; and ears have they, and eyes to see, and faith, and courage true. And glorious testimony shall they give of the light that gleamed athwart the sky as Joseph rose to oracle the Zion of the Latter-days.

"Called home by the Prophet in the Summer of 1841, the Twelve began to return from the nations. Orson Hyde, however, continued on his apostolic mission to Jerusalem, while Lorenzo Snow remained in charge of the work in London, and Parley P. Pratt remained to conduct the general affairs of the British mission in conjunction with his editorship of the *Millennial Star*.

"On the 1st of July, 1841, President Young, with Heber C. Kimball and John Taylor, arrived in Nauvoo, where they were cordially welcomed by the Prophet. Others followed. And concerning their joint work, Joseph thus summarizes:

'All the quorum of the Twelve Apostles who were expected here this season, with the exception of Willard Richards and Wilford Woodruff, have arrived. We have listened to the accounts which they give of their success, and the prosperity of the work of the Lord in Great Britain, with pleasure.

'They certainly have been instruments in the hands of God accomplishing much, and must have the satisfaction of knowing that they have done their duty. Perhaps no men ever undertook such an important mission under such peculiarly distressing, forbidding and unpropitious circumstances. Most of them, when they left this place, nearly two years ago, were worn down with sickness and disease, or were taken sick on the road. Several of their families were also afflicted, and needed their aid and support. But knowing that they had been called by the God of heaven to preach the gospel to other nations, they conferred not with flesh and blood, but, obedient to the heavenly mandate, without purse or scrip, commenced a journey of five thousand miles entirely dependent on the providence of that God who had called them to such a holy calling.

'While journeying to the seaboard they were brought into many trying circumstances. After a short recovery from severe sickness they would be taken with a relapse, and have to stop among strangers, without money and without friends. Their lives were several times despaired of, and they have taken each other by the hand, expecting it was the last time they should behold one another in the flesh.

'Notwithstanding their afflictions and trials, the Lord always interposed in their behalf, and did not suffer them to sink into the arms of death. Some way or other was made for their escape; friends rose up when they most needed them, and relieved their necessities, and thus they were enabled to pursue their journey and rejoice in the holy one of Israel. They truly went forth weeping, bearing precious seed, but have returned rejoicing, bearing their sheaves with them.'

"With this may properly be coupled the birds-eye view which Brigham Young gave of the Apostolic work in Great Britain. He said:

'It is with a heart full of thanksgiving and gratitude to God, my heavenly Father, that I reflect upon his dealings with me and my brethren of the Twelve during the past year of my life which was spent in England. It truly seems a miracle to look upon the contrast between our landing and departing from Liverpool. We landed in the Spring of 1840, as strangers in a strange land, and penniless; but through the mercy of God we have gained many friends, established churches in almost every noted town and city of Great Britain, baptized between seven and eight thousand souls, printed five thousand Books of Mormon, three thousand hymn books, two thousand five hundred volumes of the *Millenial Star,* and fifty thousand tracts; emigrated to Zion one thousand souls, establishing a permanent shipping agency, which will be a great blessing to the saints, and have left sown in the hearts of many thousands the seed of eternal life, which shall bring forth fruit to the honor and glory of God; and yet we have lacked nothing to eat, drink or wear. In all these things I acknowledge the hand of God.' . . .

"But the apostolic record of 1840-1 would be marked-ly incomplete without the strikingly suggestive and significant picture of Orson Hyde on the Mount of Olives, blessing the sacred land of the prophets, and removing from it the curse of ages. In his report from Alexandria, Egypt, Nov. 22nd, 1841, he says:

"On Sunday morning, October 24th, a good while before day, I arose from sleep and went out of the city as soon as the gates were opened, crossed the brook Cedron, and went upon the Mount of Olives and there, in solemn silence, with pen, ink and paper (just as I saw in the vision), offered up the following prayer to him who lives forever and ever:

'O Thou who art from everlasting to everlasting, eternally and unchangeably the same, even the God who rules in the heavens above, and controls the destinies of men on the earth, wilt thou not condescend, through thine infinite goodness and royal favor, to listen to the prayer of thy servant which he this day offers up unto thee in the name of thy holy child Jesus, upon this land, where the Son of Righteousness sat in blood, and thine Anointed One expired.

'Be pleased, O Lord, to forgive all the follies, weaknesses, vanities, and sins of thy servant, and strengthen him to resist all future temptations. Give him prudence and discernment that he may avoid the evil, and a heart to choose the good; give him fortitude to bear up under trying and adverse circumstances, and grace to endure all things for thy name's sake, until the end shall come, when all the saints shall rest in peace.

'Now, O Lord, thy servant has been obedient to the heavenly vision which thou gavest him in his native land; and under the shadow of thine outstretched arm, he has safely arrived in this place to dedicate and consecrate this land unto thee, for the gathering together of Judah's scattered remnants, according to the predictions of the holy prophets—for the building up of Jerusalem again after it has been trodden down by the Gentiles so long, and for rearing a temple in honor of thy name. Everlasting thanks be ascribed unto thee, O Father, Lord of heaven and earth, that Thou hast preserved thy servant from the dangers of the seas, and from the plague and pestilence which have caused the land to mourn. The violence of man has also been restrained, and thy providential care by night and by day has been exercised over thine unworthy servant. Accept, therefore, O Lord, the tribute of a grateful heart for all past favors, and be pleased to continue thy kindness and mercy towards a needy worm of the dust.

'O Thou, who didst covenant with Abraham, thy friend, and who did renew that covenant with Isaac, and confirm the same with Jacob with an oath, that thou wouldst not only give them this land for an everlasting inheritance, but that thou wouldst also remember their seed forever. Abraham, Isaac, and Jacob have long since closed their eyes in death, and made the grave their mansion. Their children are scattered and dispersed abroad among the nations of the Gentiles like sheep that have no shepherd, and are still looking forward for the fulfillment of those promises which thou didst make concerning them; and even this land, which once poured forth nature's richest bounty, and flowed, as it were, with milk and honey, has, to a certain extent, been smitten with barrenness and sterility since it drank from murderous hands the blood of him who never sinned.

'Grant, therefore, O Lord, in the name of thy well-beloved Son, Jesus Christ, to remove the barrenness and sterility of this land, and let springs of living water break forth to water its thirsty soil. Let the vine and the olive produce in their strength, and the fig tree bloom and flourish. Let the land become abundantly fruitful when possessed by its rightful heirs; let it again flow with plenty to feed the returning prodigals who come home with a spirit of grace and supplication; upon it let the clouds distil virtue and richness, and let the fields smile with plenty. Let the flocks and the herds greatly increase and multiply upon the mountains and the hills; and let thy great kindness conquer and subdue the unbelief of thy people. Do thou take from them their stony heart, and give them a heart of flesh; and may the Sun of thy favor dispel the cold mists of darkness which have beclouded their atmosphere. Incline them to gather in upon this land according to thy word. Let them come like clouds and like doves to their windows. Let the large ships of the nations bring them from the distant isles; and let kings become their nursing fathers, and queens with motherly fondness wipe the tear of sorrow from their eye.

'Thou, O Lord, didst once move upon the heart of Cyrus to show favor unto Jerusalem and her children. Do thou now also be pleased to inspire the hearts of kings and the powers of the earth to look with a friendly eye towards this place, and with a desire to see thy righteous purposes executed in relation thereto. Let them know that it is thy good pleasure to restore the kingdom unto Israel— raise up Jerusalem as its capital, and constitute her people a distinct nation and government, with David thy servant, even a descendant from the loins of ancient David, to be their king.

'Let that nation or that people who shall take an active part in behalf of Abraham's children, and in the raising up of Jerusalem, find favor in thy sight. Let not their enemies prevail against them, neither let pestilence or famine overcome them, but let the glory of Israel overshadow them, and the power of the highest protect them; while that nation or kingdom that will not serve thee in this glorious work must perish, according to thy word — 'Yea, those nations shall be utterly wasted.' "

*   *   *   *   *   *   *

"Is not this a magnificent illustration of the subject and themes presented previously? What a picture is this of the 'Times of the Restitution,' spoken of by the ancient prophets! It is a prophecy, in the very action of the age, of the 'New and Everlasting Covenant,' to be made by Jehovah with all Israel."

*   *   *   *   *   *   *

And now let us turn to the "very action of the age," described by Tullidge's gifted pen (pages 287 and 288).

"Then Joseph . . . one day in the temple (Kirtland) . . . . . . went over to Heber C. Kimball, in whom he knew the Spirit dwelt, and declared, 'The Spirit whispers to me, Let my servant Heber take a mission to Great Britain, to open the door of salvation to that nation.'"

Not long after his arrival in fulfillment of that call 'The answer which Heber sent back across the waters, in that day, was

'Glory to God Joseph! The Lord is with us among the nations abroad!' "

Twenty years later (JD 6:190, Dec. 27, 1857) he recalled:

" 'I recollect being in England, in the town of Chadburn, Lancashire; and while there I felt as if my whole system was alive; I felt quickened by some unseen power. Brother Hyde was with me, and he knows that it is true;

and I felt to pull off my shoes. We pulled off our hats, for we felt such a sacred and holy feeling. I told Brother Joseph about it when I came home and he said 'Brother Heber, that place was dedicated by one of the old Prophets and it will always be filled with the spirit of life'. . . I wish . . . you were all as visionary as those holy men were who dedicated these places in the days of Jesus and the Apostles.' "

(See pages 61 to 63 and III Nephi 16: 1-5 and 17:1-4)

Returning to Tullidge's inspiring exposition of this eternal theme:

"Now was the grand spiritual test to be put to *all nations* and to *every creature*,—the test which has been given only by Jesus and Joseph. Will it fail? Ah! that is the problem, even to this day, one which millions, in the near future, (now a century nearer) are going to prove for themselves!"

May the Lord God of Israel make us equal to the test!

INDEX

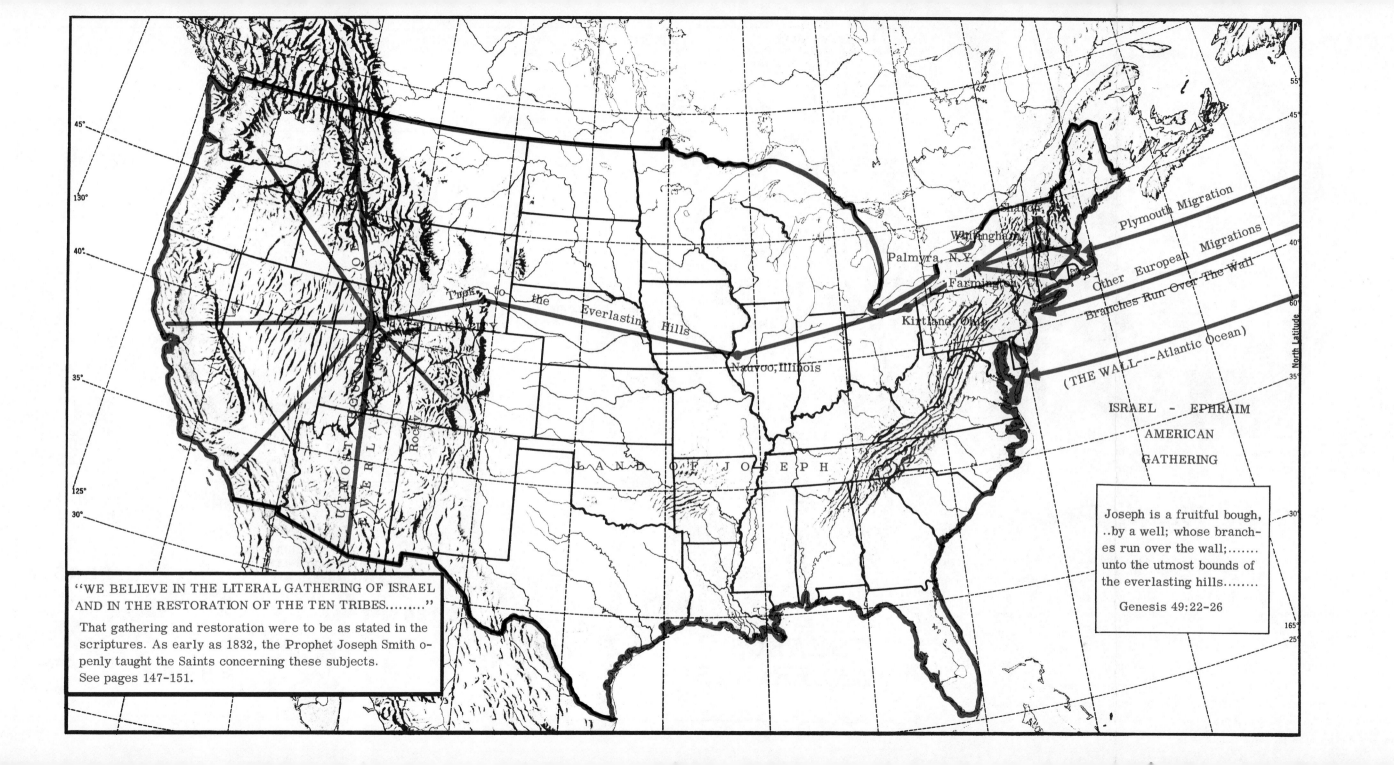

Plymouth Migration

Other European Migrations

Branches Run Over The Wall

(THE WALL---Atlantic Ocean)

ISRAEL - EPHRAIM

AMERICAN

GATHERING

North Latitude

Palmyra, N.Y.

Whitingham

Sharon

Farmington

Kirtland, Ohio

Trek to the Everlasting Hills

Nauvoo, Illinois

SALT LAKE CITY

L A N D   O F   J O S E P H

Rocky

Joseph is a fruitful bough,
..by a well; whose branches run over the wall;.......
unto the utmost bounds of
the everlasting hills........

Genesis 49:22-26

"WE BELIEVE IN THE LITERAL GATHERING OF ISRAEL
AND IN THE RESTORATION OF THE TEN TRIBES........."

That gathering and restoration were to be as stated in the
scriptures. As early as 1832, the Prophet Joseph Smith o-
penly taught the Saints concerning these subjects.
See pages 147-151.

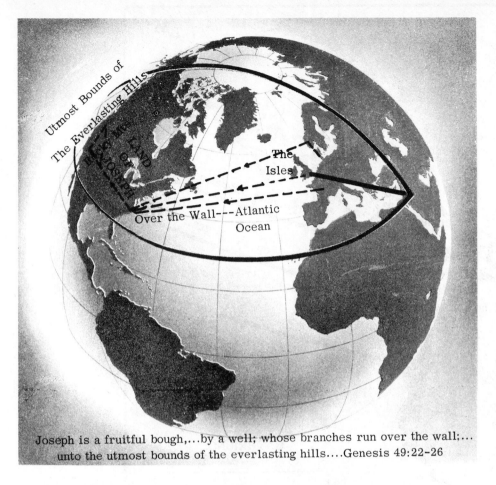

Utmost Bounds of
The Everlasting Hills

The Isles

Over the Wall----Atlantic
Ocean

Joseph is a fruitful bough,...by a well; whose branches run over the wall;...
unto the utmost bounds of the everlasting hills....Genesis 49:22-26

North and West of Palestine

The wilderness of the people, where the House of Israel, in exile from Palestine, were to grow and expand into a great people and company of nations, and where also they were to find grace in the sight of the Lord (Jer. 31: 2), is defined by Isaiah as north and west of Palestine (Isa. 49: 8–12).

Critics who object to the use of the prophet's reference to the *north and west* as locating the Isles northwest of Palestine cannot logi-

cally object to a literal application of Isaiah's boundaries to define a larger section of the globe as shown above. It is in the territory thus bounded by north and west directional lines, running from a point in Palestine and intersecting at a point in the Pacific Ocean west of the coast of the United States of America, that the activity of the modern House of Israel is found today.

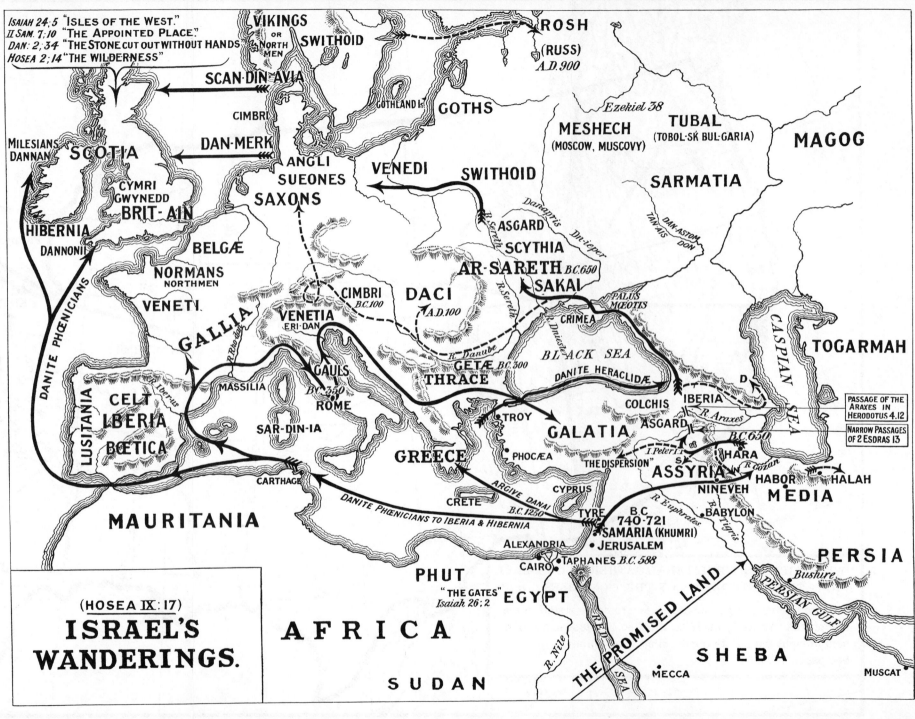

ISAIAH 24;5 "ISLES OF THE WEST."
II SAM. 7;10 "THE APPOINTED PLACE."
DAN: 2, 34 "THE STONE CUT OUT WITHOUT HANDS."
HOSEA 2;14 "THE WILDERNESS"

VIKINGS OR NORTH MEN — SWITHOID

ROSH (RUSS) A.D.900

SCAN-DIN-AVIA

CIMBRI   GOTHLAND IS.   GOTHS

Ezekiel 38   TUBAL (TOBOL-SK BUL-GARIA)   MAGOG

MESHECH (MOSCOW, MUSCOVY)

DAN-MERK

ANGLI   VENEDI   SWITHOID   SARMATIA

Milesians Dannan   SCOTIA   SUEONES   SAXONS

CYMRI GWYNEDD   BRIT-AIN

R.Sereth   ASGARD   SCYTHIA   Danapris   Dnieper   DAN-ASTOM DON   TANAIS

AR-SARETH B.C.650   SAKAI

HIBERNIA   BELGÆ

DANNONII   NORMANS NORTHMEN   CIMBRI B.C.100   DACI A.D.100   R.Sereth   PALUS MŒOTIS

VENETI   R.Danube   CRIMEA   TOGARMAH

GALLIA   VENETIA ERI-DAN   GETÆ B.C.300   BLACK SEA   DANITE HERACLIDÆ   CASPIAN SEA

GAULS   THRACE   D

DANITE PHŒNICIANS   R.Rhodanus   MASSILIA   B.C.350 ROME   TROY   COLCHIS   IBERIA   PASSAGE OF THE ARAXES IN HERODOTUS 4.12

LUSITANIA   CELT IBERIA   SAR-DIN-IA   GALATIA   ASGARD   R.Araxes   NARROW PASSAGES OF 2 ESDRAS 13

BŒTICA   Iberus   PHOCÆA   B.C.650

GREECE   "THE DISPERSION"   I Peter 1;1   HARA   ASSYRIA   R.Gozan

CARTHAGE   ARGIVE DANAI   CYPRUS   NINEVEH   HABOR   HALAH   MEDIA

DANITE PHŒNICIANS TO IBERIA & HIBERNIA   CRETE   B.C.1250   TYRE   B.C. 740-721 SAMARIA (KHUMRI)   Babylon   R.Euphrates   Tigris

MAURITANIA   ALEXANDRIA   JERUSALEM   PERSIA

CAIRO   TAPHANES B.C.588   Bushire

PHUT   "THE GATES" Isaiah 26;2   PERSIAN GULF

(HOSEA IX:17)   "THE GATES" Isaiah 26;2 EGYPT   THE PROMISED LAND

ISRAEL'S WANDERINGS.

AFRICA   R.Nile   RED SEA   SHEBA

SUDAN   MECCA   MUSCAT

CHARLES DICKENS CAME TO SCOFF BUT WROTE WORDS OF PRAISE ABOUT THE EMIGRANT SAINTS.

Early in the history of the Latter-day Saint church a mighty gathering was taking place. England furnished thousands of converts. The movement was widely known and discussed.

Charles Dickens, too, was more than passively curious. One day, with a story in mind, he boarded the "packet" ship *Amazon*. As Mr. "Uncommercial" he wrote about what he saw. Here is some of it:

"Behold me on my way to an Eimgrant Ship on a hot morning early in June . . .

"I go aboard my Emigrant ship . . . But nobody is in an ill temper, nobody is the worse for drink, nobody swears an oath or uses a coarse word, nobody appears depressed, nobody is weeping, and down upon the deck in every corner where it is possible to find a few square feet to kneel, crouch, or lie in, people in every unsuitable attitude for writing, are writing letters.

"Now, I have been in emigrant ships before this day in June. And these people are *so strikingly different from all* other people in like circumstances whom I have ever seen, that I wonder aloud, 'What would a stranger suppose these emigrants to be!'

"The vigilant bright face of the weather-browned captain of the *Amazon* is at my shoulder, and he says, 'What, indeed! The most of these came aboard yesterday evening. They came from various parts of England in small parties that had never seen one another before. *Yet they had not been a couple of hours on board, when they established their own police, made their own regulations, and set their own watches at all the hatchways.* Before nine o'clock, the ship was as orderly and as quiet as a man of war! . . .